MINING GROUP GOLD®

How to Cash in on the Collaborative Brain Power of a Group

Second Edition

THOMAS A. KAYSER

McGraw-Hill

New York San Francisco Washington, D.C. Auckland Bogotá
Caracas Lisbon London Madrid Mexico City Milan
Montreal New Delhi San Juan Singapore
Sydney Tokyo Toronto

McGraw-Hill

A Division of The McGraw·Hill Companies

Library of Congress Cataloging-in-Publication Data

Kayser, Thomas A., 1942–
   Mining Group Gold : how to cash in on the collaborative brain
power of a group / Thomas A. Kayser. — 2nd ed.
     p.   cm.
   Includes bibliographical references and index.
   ISBN 0-7863-0429-4
   1. Work groups. 2. Problem solving, Group. I. Title.
HD66.K39 1996
658.4'036—dc20   95–2846

Printed in the United States of America
13 14 15 QWV/QWV 0 9 8 7

FOREWORD

"It must be considered that there is nothing more difficult to carry out, nor more doubtful of success, nor more dangerous to handle than to initiate a new order of things."

Machiavelli

Initiating a new order of things is, indeed, difficult to do. For us today, initiating is merely the first step. Change is not a discrete event, which once initiated, can be finished. It is a continuous process always evolving and moving toward something different. Cultural change is, perhaps, the most important responsibility of management.

American business, education, nonprofit organizations, and even government have come to recognize that success and competitiveness constantly require new approaches. As each new focus (total quality, time-to-market, reengineering, for example) energizes an enterprise, it helps improve the bottom-line and the productivity of that organization. But each new focus also requires that roles, responsibilities, and working relationships be adjusted and renegotiated. As important as a new direction is, equally important is the new work organization and the new work process—the new culture—that is required. Enterprises today are faced with having to define a process that will enable the simultaneous accomplishment of productivity, effectiveness, and quality improvements while maintaining a steady course in the achievement of corporate goals like customer satisfaction, market share, employee satisfaction, and return on assets. When defined, it is this process which must then become the very basis and cultural underpinning of the organization.

The process of managing people and ideas to achieve a high level of results in a complex, turbulent, global economy is what *Mining Group Gold* is all about. It is a practical, easy to apply guide to changing the culture through building and maintaining collaboration within and across work teams. This book clearly defines the tools and processes that can make a difference in team productivity, and it applies to any environment. *Mining Group Gold* can be used by any team concerned with accomplishing a task and willing to involve individuals in the group toward reaching a solution.

These tools emphasize teamwork and the building of consensus through careful planning and team facilitation. The contents of this book walk the reader through the process from initial planning to actually facilitating collaborative work sessions. It outlines the steps to be followed and the behaviors required to ensure teamwork and positive responses. The concentration on implementation and "how to" makes this book uniquely useful.

Tom Kayser knows his material. He is one of a handful of Xerox people who has spent over a decade working exclusively on evolving a new style and approach to doing business. It is this approach which enabled the Xerox Corporation's achievement of the 1989 Malcolm Baldrige National Quality Award and the winning of national quality awards in eighteen other countries. It is this new approach which has since been instrumental in assuring new products and improved profits. While strategic direction has evolved and refocused, and our Corporate vision has solidified, the methodology described by Kayser has been consistently utilized. Throughout major organizational changes, and experiments with decentralization, divisionalization, and delayering, the constant focus on collaboration as outlined in this book assured that bottom-line results would be achieved. You cannot overestimate the value of the collaborative process.

That, simply, is what *Mining Group Gold* is all about. It is mastery of the collaboration process which allows people to control events, determine solutions, and produce meaningful results. *Mining Group Gold* is easy to understand and implement. It applies to any group, in any environment.

Although our journey is not over, it is satisfying now to stand back and look at the significant cultural changes Xerox has made. But it hasn't been easy going through them. *Mining Group Gold* has made a difference. It has provided a roadmap through uncharted territory by outlining a collaborative philosophy and approach we could hold on to. I hope you find the tools, tips, and techniques in this book as useful, as powerful, and as simple to implement as we have. They work. And because they do, I know that you will be pleased with the changes that result.

Deborah K. Smith
Vice President and Director, Corporate Employee Resources
Xerox Corporation

PREFACE

The football team of Augustana College in Rock Island, Illinois has an offensive playbook that is so simple it can be diagrammed on a napkin. It contains only six running plays and four passing plays! Rival coaches admit: "Augustana knows that you know what they've got. But their execution is terrific." It's so terrific that in the twelve seasons from 1983 through 1994, Augustana built a record of 114–15–1 and won four NCAA Division III championships. And yet, Coach Bob Reade and his staff are not afraid to recruit players to start as freshman and sophomores because their plays are so simple.

This book is analogous to Augustana's football playbook; it contains only the significant few plays. Learning to do these well—to have terrific execution of the fundamental principles—will increase your ability to plan and lead productive group sessions to an extent you did not think possible. Although I am familiar with much of the research and literature on facilitation, collaboration, teams, and teamwork, this book is neither a compilation nor a summarization of that material. It's more—much more.

Mining Group Gold is an integrated approach for thinking strategically about the management of people in group sessions. It is a book of team leadership and behavior. Specifically, *Mining Group Gold* is a set of fundamental—but potent—tools, principles, techniques, and guidesheets that any person, at any organizational level, can easily apply to increase his or her ability to plan and facilitate work sessions that build a collaborative organization. I have successfully used these procedures in all types of group situations over the past 15 years.

Subsequently, I have discovered that managing efficient and effective collaborative sessions comprises a set of skills you must deliberately set out to acquire. I'm convinced that the necessary skills are the relatively simple ones presented in this book. However something Franklin D. Roosevelt once said about introducing new ideas into government applies here. "New ideas," said FDR, "cannot be administered successfully by men with old ideas, for the first essential of doing a job well is the wish to see it done at all."

Without your desire to do it, the ideas presented in this book are useless. You are completely in charge of what this book will ultimately mean to you and your organization. There is nothing complicated here. You do not have to be a group dynamics expert or a seasoned facilitator to make these tools and processes work for you. No theories. No formulas. Rather, some concise, easy-to-understand information that will put you on the leading edge of common sense—just six "running plays" and four "passing plays."

As the title suggests, by reading and practicing the ideas presented in this book, you will learn how to mine the gold nuggets of wisdom brought to the session by each participant so everyone can cash in on the collaborative brain power of the group.

WHAT YOU WILL LEARN FROM THIS BOOK

This is a book on how to organize and facilitate collaborative team sessions. It is *not* a book on how to become a master of meeting politics, how to crush your opponent, how to dominate a session and get your own way, or how to win at the expense of others.

The framework for *Mining Group Gold* is built around 14 principals. Besides assimilating the 14 principles, you will learn how to execute them through a number of fundamental actions: five steps for successfully planning the structure of a session, three alternatives for opening a team session, five options for enhancing the productivity of the middle of the session, and four easy steps for significantly increasing the power of the session's close. You will become fully acquainted with a set of group task and maintenance behaviors and learn their role in work group facilitation. Also, you will gain knowledge about how to initiate a collaborative climate and how to maintain it, how to constructively deal with feelings, how to manage group conflict, how to handle disruptive behavior, how to reduce confusion, and more.

When you have finished this book, you will have learned how to be more accomplished in the art of managing people and ideas during work sessions to achieve agreed to desired outcomes. You will have acquired the group strategies necessary to carry you and your organization across the goal line.

SOME THOUGHTS TO KEEP IN MIND

As you read *Mining Group Gold*, please keep the following points in mind.

➤ While the focus of this book is geared to the perspective of the manager facilitating his or her work group, these techniques are applicable to a variety of group situations. Any person responsible for leading any type of group session will find this material relevant and valuable.

➤ To obtain the greatest benefit from *Mining Group Gold*, read it straight through to gain an overall view of each chapter and, in turn, the flow of the whole book. During this initial reading, highlight key points that are of particular interest, then go back to those points for a more detailed review and study. Write a final set of notes to yourself on the Notes Worksheet at the end of each chapter.

➤ The points presented here are not ironclad rules and regulations. Rather, they are ideas for guiding you in practicing the art of excellent team facilitation and leadership.

➤ Finally, because these are only guidelines, you are encouraged to initially practice the techniques and processes as described. However, after gaining experience and confidence in their use, supplement and refine this foundation in order to increase your skill in building a collaborative team.

USING THESE IDEAS IN A WORK ENVIRONMENT

The key to success in acquiring or improving your team leadership is the old refrain: practice, practice, practice. There are no shortcuts. However, skill development can be an organized endeavor using *Mining Group Gold* as your central resource. The skill acquisition process involves a series of successive approximations: planning the structure and process of the group session; facilitating the session; assessing—with the help of everyone present—where the session went well and where it did not go well; making a new plan that preserves the positive aspects of the previous effort while reducing or eliminating the negative aspects; and then trying again. With each cycle, the group will make progress in its ability to pull together and will soon realize that everyone on the team, not only the leader, shares responsibility for successful facilitation.

You will discover that the art of team leadership is rewarding. It is a powerful lever in building the collaborative culture so necessary to accomplishing the tough tasks that lie ahead. Equally important, facilitation done well heightens job satisfaction for you, as well as for the members of your team, by unleashing greater accomplishment in an environment of trust, collaboration, and commitment.

Above all else do not regard an unsuccessful facilitation effort as a failure; instead consider it as another opportunity to try again—more intelligently.

A FINAL WORD

To avoid getting into a writer's rut, I have used the terms *manager, group manager, administrator, group leader, supervisor, task-force chairperson,* and *committee chairperson* interchangeably. These terms merely signify the person responsible for setting up and conducting work related meetings. Throughout this book, the person referred to as initiating a team session should always be thought of as the primary facilitator. This means besides being involved in meeting content, the person initiating the session also has another primary interest: helping the assembled collection of people function well as a team.

Now it is time to begin our journey to explore and understand the richly rewarding process of facilitation excellence.

Acknowledgments

As with any endeavor of this nature, there are numerous people who have contributed to *Mining Group Gold* both intellectually and emotionally. First of all, I extend my thanks to all of the talented Xerox managers and individual contributors I have had the privilege of interacting with as the first edition of *Mining Group Gold* gained widespread acceptance throughout the corporation. You praised; you questioned; you challenged; you suggested; you moved me to expand, to sharpen, and to refine my thinking about the tools and processes I was advocating. But most of all you applied the ideas and concepts back on the job. You proved beyond any doubt that they work and that the facilitation of collaborative sessions is within the reach of any group willing to learn and consistently practice a few fundamental principles. Without your influence and endorsement there would be no second edition.

A special thank you must go to my wife, Carol, for her many useful suggestions for revising the content of the chapters based on her extensive experience using this material with her consulting clients.

My appreciation is given to Donald Zrebiec for his friendly, but relentless hounding to "get off the dime" and just write the darn thing (the first edition) because the subject matter and methodology is critical to business success. I am grateful to Ron Cox, Tom McMullen, Tim Tyler, Bob Kelsch, and Jean Beasley for listening when I needed it most and for being excellent ambassadors for my work.

I am appreciative of the work and consultation that John Hansen provided on Chapter 9. Also, my thanks go to David Jones for his insightful comments on the first edition.

Colleen Bonar, Mark Bower, Phil Chirico, Ann Delehant, Meg Keller–Cogan, Robert McKanna, Harv Paris, Diane Reed, Tom Flood, Josephine Kehoe, and Roger Gorham all must be recognized for their advocacy and proactive efforts to infuse the principles and philosophy of *Mining Group Gold* into the school districts of Rochester, New York, and a number of surrounding towns.

I owe much gratitude to Jeff Krames, Publisher of McGraw-Hill Professional Publishing, for believing in this material and being passionate about publishing a second edition.

Finally, to my son Chad, my deepest appreciation for keeping your Thursday evening schedule open—even when inconvenient—so we could have "boys night out" to be together and just talk. When I first sat down to begin writing the first edition of *Mining Group Gold*, you were 10 years old and in fifth grade; now, as I finish the second edition, you are 17 and will be going to college next year. Each of us has grown and learned over the course of this project, but you have had, by far, the richest learning experience as you have grown from boy to young man.

CONTENTS

3. THE KEY TO THE GOLD MINE: FACILITATION · 34

4. PLANNING THE STRUCTURE OF A SESSION TO MINE GROUP GOLD: FIVE STEPS TO SUCCESS · 49

5. PLANNING THE PROCESS OF A SESSION TO MINE GROUP GOLD: THREE PHASES TO SUCCESS

6. INTERPERSONAL BEHAVIORS FOR MINING GROUP GOLD: A SHARED RESPONSIBILITY

CHAPTER ONE

MINING GROUP GOLD: INTEGRATING THE PAST WITH A VISION OF THE FUTURE

CHAPTER OBJECTIVES

➤ To provide a retrospective look at the roots and evolution of *Mining Group Gold* over the past dozen years.

➤ To highlight the *14 Principles of Mining Group Gold* that have crystallized from applying the strategies and techniques from the first edition.

➤ To take a look at the future of facilitation, collaboration, and teamwork.

INTRODUCTION

A dozen years! Unbelievable to me, but that's how long it has been since I first became involved in a seemingly short-term project at Xerox in 1983 that now has evolved and grown into the second edition of this book. The terrain of facilitation experience I have covered during the past 12 years has been both vast and varied. Lessons have been learned, group session structures and processes have been honed, and a philosophy about how to cash in on the collaborative brain power of a team has been confirmed.

At the dawning of the 1980s, the external market place, the business and economic climate, and the values of American managers about the art of successful management were immensely different from today. Looking back, it's easy to see how American organizations at that time—in both the public and private sector—had self-selected themselves into three categories.

Category one contained the few American companies, like Xerox, that were just beginning to awake from their deep slumber of complacency and to realize that they had to change the fundamental way they did business in order to become a world class competitor in a new, global economy.

Category two contained firms in industries such as steel and autos that scurried to hide behind the fortress of government tariffs and regulations as their protection against the onslaught of worldwide competition.

Category three contained everyone else—the overwhelming majority of government and business organizations. All of these organizations felt comfortable and secure as they whistled past the graveyard. "Change? Who needs change? Our bureaucratic systems, policies, procedures, and management style have worked for us since the beginning of time. Why transform anything now? We'll do what's always worked before. We'll downsize, cut costs, and everything will be fine."

That was the reality of the early 80s. However, reflecting on the 12-year journey I've personally covered with Xerox, and reviewing the general literature on organizational behavior and change, I'm struck by one simple but overwhelming fact—the more things change, the more they remain the same. *I'm convinced now, more than ever, that the one constant in the wrenching change to become a world class competitor in the global economy, the single road over which "the new order of things" rides, is collaboration and its facilitation within and across work teams!*

THE ROOTS OF MINING GROUP GOLD

To better understand why I am so adamant in my belief, we need to begin by tracing the roots of this second edition of *Mining Group Gold.*

My first attempts as an internal process consultant within the Business Products & Systems Group (BP&SG) of Xerox in 1982 were very frustrating. Initially the culture was extremely resistant. My mere suggestion of planning the structure and process of group sessions, initiating and maintaining a collaborative climate in meetings, acknowledging and understanding the feelings of others, sharing power, working in teams, searching for consensus, or building win/win solutions was enough to send many managers into a tirade that would leave my ears ringing for hours.

A few visionary managers did see the power of teamwork and collaboration and enlisted my help in turning their work groups into teams. These initial efforts—and the hands-on learning that came from them—while far from division wide, provided information and data that would prove invaluable later on. It was tough, slow, in-the-trenches work. But soon a confluence of internal and external circumstances would change all of that. The whole corporation was about to be thrust into a race for its life—a marathon on a global race track that even today keeps reconfiguring itself and has no finish line.

Back in the 1982–83 time frame, Xerox was a bruised and battered company. Let David Kearns, chief executive officer of Xerox from 1982 to 1990, candidly describe the situation he faced at the beginning of his tenure at the helm.

> To many in the outside world, we still looked very much like the invincible copier giant and bedrock of the *Fortune 500* that we had always been. It was evident that we were having a few problems. But still, we were making hundreds of millions of dollars a year. We were turning out fresh products. We were employing a hundred thousand people. How bad could things be?
>
> Unfortunately, I knew. We were gravely sick. . . A lot of our problems boiled down to the Japanese. They were really eating us for lunch.

3

> One thing I gleaned [from over two dozen trips to Japan] was that the Japanese had consciously made the decision to select our company as a "target"... They had good reason to do so; they were selling products for what it cost us to make them. Our market share had tumbled from more than 90 percent in the early 1970s to less than 15 percent. Every year, competitors nibbled away a few more share points. We were being decimated. Whether we liked it or not, we were in a war to the death. . . . How bad off were we? To put it bluntly, if nothing were done to correct things, we were destined to have a fire sale and close down by 1990.
>
> Our only hope for survival was to urgently commit ourselves to vastly improving the quality of our products and service . . . It meant changing the very culture of Xerox from the ground up . . . In our near-death situation, I felt we had no choice but to accomplish this.[1]

It was apparent that for a significant cultural change based on total quality was to succeed, the highest levels of management would have to own it. Kearns, with the help of outside consultant David Nadler, spent the bulk of 1983 working hand in hand with the corporation's 25 senior operating executives from around the world. They hammered out a quality policy and the broad outlines of a quality strategy and implementation plan. All of this was given the name: Leadership Through Quality. Once the broad plans were in place, several senior level quality improvement teams were formed to flesh out the myriad details.

In April of 1984, I participated in training the senior staff of the Business Products & Systems Group (BP&SG) as we became the first division in Xerox to commence the required cultural change. The nature and scope of this change can be shown by contrasting the culture of Xerox back then with the state the company has achieved today.

- Movement from unstructured and individualistic problem solving and decision making to disciplined and predominately collaborative efforts.

- Movement from an ambiguous or incomplete understanding of customer requirements to the use of a systematic, interactive approach to fully understanding customer needs and requirements.

- Movement from acceptance of a certain margin of error and subsequent corrective action as the norm, to an environment in which we collaborate within and across functions for error free outputs that fully satisfy customer requirements the first time.

This new direction clearly put a premium on group-oriented behaviors and actions. Teamwork and collaboration were then, and are even more so today, the road over which the company's never-ending transformation continues to ride.

However, as we began the initial roll-out of Leadership Through Quality in the Business Products & Systems Group (BP&SG) in early 1984, few managers, or senior professionals responsible for chairing committees or task forces, truly understood the basics of planning the structure and process of a group session. Even fewer cared about the fundamentals of facilitating a collaborative session where power is shared with the whole group, the wisdom of everyone is systematically processed in an open trusting way, and consensus is used at appropriate opportunities to make decisions. Unfortunately, this lack of understanding and commitment to collaborative processes was the standard bill of fare for most of American business, industry, and government at that time.

Participative management, or Theory Y as it was labeled then, was dismissed as a soft, "touchy feely," country club approach to running things. Hardball was the only game in town. If you were good at it, you were viewed as a winner and your career blossomed. If you weren't good at it, or chose not to play that game, you were branded a loser and your career withered.

A most vivid account of this intimidating, autocratic, power-oriented style in action, and the culture it created, is provided by David Halberstam in his Pulitzer Prize winning book, *The Best and the Brightest.* It is a book about the involvement of the United States in the war in Vietnam. Regardless of your feelings about that war, the interactive processes used by Robert S. McNamara, the Secretary of Defense under both Presidents Kennedy and Johnson during that period, are quite instructive.

5

Those who attended the meetings learned how to play the game; the McNamara requests to speak freely were not to be taken too seriously. He would telegraph his own viewpoint, more often than not unconsciously, in the way he expressed the problem, and in particular he would summarize in an intimidating way, outlining point by point, using the letters of the alphabet, A through J, if necessary, and his position always seemed to win out in the summation. If you dissented or deviated, he listened, but you could almost hear the fingers wanting to drum on the table; if you agreed and gave pro evidence, he would respond warmly, his voice approving in tone. Gradually those who disagreed learned their lesson, and just as gradually he would reach out to men who were like him until he was surrounded by men in his own image. Those who knew him well could tell when he was angry, when he was going to explode. He would become tense, and if you looked under the table you could begin to see him hitch up his pants, a nervous habit, done because he knew he could not control his hands if they were on the table. The more restless he became, the more his antagonist assaulted his senses, the higher the pants would get, showing thick hairy legs. On bad days the pants might reach to his knees, and then suddenly he would talk, bang, bang, bang. You're wrong for these reasons. Flicking his fingers out. One. Two. Three. . . He always ran out of fingers.[2]

When it came right down to it, McNamara had doubts about the bombing [of Vietnam] in his mind, but those doubts were not reflected in the meetings. He was forceful, intense, tearing apart the doubts of others, almost ruthless in making his case; those around him were sure he was being encouraged by the President [Lyndon B. Johnson] to do this; he was too much the corporate man to go as far as he did without somehow sensing that this was his role. He was, as [George] Ball [Under Secretary of State for Economic Affairs] found, quite different in private sessions than in the major meetings where Johnson presided. When Ball prepared paper after paper for Johnson, he would first send them to the other principals, and occasionally McNamara would suggest that he come by and talk the paper over before they went to see the President. Ball would find McNamara surprisingly sympathetic, indeed there seemed to be a considerable area of agreement. Sometimes John McNaughton [Aide to McNamara, expert on arms control, and former Harvard Law School professor] was present and McNamara would note that McNaughton was in general agreement with Ball, that he had great doubts about the course they were following. So Ball often left feeling that he had made some impression, that he had stirred some doubts in McNamara, that there was the beginning of an area of agreement. But then, in the real meetings, with Johnson present, it would be quite different: McNamara the ripper now, his own doubts having disappeared, could not afford to lose an argument, or even express partial doubt; partial sympathy for Ball might hurt his own case. So he plunged forward, leaving Ball somewhat surprised and dominated by his force, his control, and his statistics. McNamara may have realized that there was an enormous element of chance to what he was proposing, that he was only for it 60–40, but it seemed at the meetings that he was for it 100 percent.[3]

These two passages are an incisive description of the philosophy, culture, and management style that has been the underpinnings of American business and government throughout this century. While this approach to running organizations still exists in abundance today, it is a strategy for failure. Dominating, power hungry egos setting a culture of intimidation, fear, and non-collaboration may ring up some short-term successes. But, in the long run, how can any organization survive as a healthy, vibrant entity if it continually abuses and destroys the *most valuable* competitive advantage that it possesses—the collaborative brain power of its people? My short answer is that it can't.

Before the launch of Leadership Through Quality, Xerox was no different than most organizations in terms of our general meeting effectiveness, collaboration, and teamwork.

7

Shortly after BP&SG began the cascade of Leadership Through Quality in April 1984, we discovered how glaring the problem was. The lack of team facilitation skills among many senior and upper-middle managers quickly became evident as a major barrier to the successful implementation of our quality strategy. Without managers at the middle and top changing their behavior and style from "order-giver" to "facilitator," we knew changing the culture would prove impossible as we moved lower in the division. In order to help the managers and senior professionals within BP&SG learn the primary tools and processes for planning and conducting productive, team-oriented, collaborative work sessions, I was asked to write an internal handbook on this subject.

After discussing my project with over seventy people, ranging from vice-presidents to first line managers, their requirements were made clear. The handbook had to:

➤ Present practical, easy-to-understand and simple-to-apply tools and processes that would make a difference in group session productivity.

➤ Be "stand alone." A training program would not be required; a thorough reading of the material would allow an individual to begin implementing the tools and processes.

➤ Reinforce the tenets and philosophy of Leadership Through Quality.

➤ Be tightly written, user friendly, and interesting.

With these requirements met, the handbook was distributed to 1,200 managers, project leaders, and senior professionals within BP&SG during the fourth quarter of 1984. Soon thereafter, requests for copies began to come in from organizations outside BP&SG, as well as from people within BP&SG who were not part of the first distribution. By October of 1990, when the first edition of the *Mining Group Gold* textbook was published, more than 14,000 copies of the original handbook had been distributed throughout Xerox, including Europe, Latin America, Mexico, Canada, and the Pacific Basin.

The first edition of *Mining Group Gold* emerged as a significantly revised and expanded version of the core material from the original handbook. It also included new approaches and insights based on the direct knowledge and experience I gained between 1984 and 1990.

For the second edition, my enhancements and additions have been drawn from five sources during the intervening years since 1990: (1) continued insights gained from conducting several hundred more team-building workshops, *Mining Group Gold* seminars, and third party facilitation activities inside of Xerox; (2) interactions with Xerox managers and senior professionals actively applying the tools and processes in a wide variety of situations; (3) knowledge my wife, Carol, has gathered from consulting with her business and education clients on the *Mining Group Gold* material; (4) feedback from users of the first edition of the book; and (5) review of the business literature.

The dominant message received from those exposed to *Mining Group Gold* has been as follows: "These tools, processes, and techniques are easy to apply; they work; we're pulling together now, we are able to build collective meaning that focuses on improving employee and customer satisfaction." Therefore, all revisions for the second edition have been made in the spirit of continuous improvement while still remaining true to the substantial customer requirements laid down by the Xerox managers in 1984.

14 COLLABORATIVE PRINCIPLES

It's gratifying to be able to say, unequivocally, that the fundamentals delivered in the first edition not only have stood the test of time over a wide variety of organizational environments and conditions but have evolved into a number of collaborative principles. These principles form the framework of the book and clearly define how collaboration can be facilitated within and across work teams.

1. **Primary facilitation rests with the person who calls the people together.** If you initiate the meeting, you

must assume the non-negotiable responsibility of being the primary defense against the propagation of a wasteful session by taking on the role of "primary facilitator" [Chapter 3].

2. **Secondary facilitation is a shared task.** This principle links directly to number one. Everyone in attendance must team up with the primary facilitator in the complimentary role of secondary facilitators. Without this joint effort, the potential for collaboration significantly diminishes [Chapter 3].

3. **Primary facilitation does not preempt extensive content contributions.** The primary facilitator always has the opportunity to be an active contributor to the content of the team session. Principle number two, shared facilitation, is the key to allowing this to happen. However, since the primary facilitator often is the manager of the team, or a person of influence running a task force or committee, verbally "switching hats" to signal a distinction between content and facilitation contributions is essential to avoid role confusion in the minds of the group members [Chapter 3].

4. **Facilitate collaboration authentically.** Attempting to manipulate these tools and processes into a command-and-control style won't work. Giving people "a feeling of collaboration," by first asking them for their inputs, so you can tell them their ideas aren't any good, and then telling them what you really intended to do all along, is inauthentic facilitation. The ability to conduct a truly collaborative session always rests on your personal credibility and integrity. When your credibility is shot, you cannot facilitate collaboration. You can only accomplish things through fear, intimidation, and brute force [Chapter 3].

5. **Begin every team session with PDORA—no exceptions.** The four tickets for admission that the primary facilitator must have in hand before convening a group session are: the session's purpose [P]; the session's desired outcomes [DO]; a process for

determining who will play the roles [R] of timekeeper, minute taker, and scribe—in addition to their standard secondary facilitator role; and an agenda [A] with clock times. Without these admission tickets in hand each time, every time, the primary facilitator is gate-crashing and should be stopped from holding the session [Chapter 4].

6. **Invite only the smallest number of people necessary to achieve the session's desired outcomes.** If you don't do this, you will create meeting Hell. You will end up filling a conference room with people who have little or nothing to say, but who will take an eternity to say it [Chapter 4].

7. **Plan,** *in advance,* **the process roadmap for achieving the stated desired outcomes.** A streamlined structured process, that outlines the means for hitting the desired outcome(s) target, is as essential to facilitating a collaborative group session as the storyboard is to making a successful movie. It is through a pre-planned structured process that you ensure an efficient collaborative session will be proactively facilitated [Chapter 5].

8. **Conduct a relevant process check at the end of every session.** Continuous improvement in group session effectiveness depends on holding regular end-of-session performance assessments focused on the specifics of the team processes and interpersonal behaviors employed [Chapter 5].

9. **Establish all 15 interpersonal behaviors and the two gate-keeping processes as standard groundrules for all sessions.** I repeatedly have been amazed by the marked improvement in collaboration, teamwork, and general meeting effectiveness once all members understand and begin practicing these basic behaviors. Also, particular emphasis by everyone on seeking information and opinions, testing comprehension, and summarizing will immeasurably enhance shared facilitation [Chapter 6].

10. **Don't duck emotions in group sessions.** I've learned that emotions are not something managers, team leaders, or team members are comfortable facilitating. That is understandable. Still, it must be done to preserve teamwork and collaboration. While you are never asked to agree with the emotions being expressed, you must never deny people the feelings they are expressing [Chapter 7].

11. **Initiating a collaborative climate in a team session is the primary facilitator's responsibility.** It is incumbent on the primary facilitator to initiate a collaborative climate by first setting the stage for information processing and then, while withholding his or her views, encouraging the open expressions of thoughts among all others present. George Odiorne describes what happens if this principle is violated: "There's a law of administration which I'd suggest holds true in almost every situation. That is, if the boss presents his solution first and then asks for opinions about it, a vote of approval will follow almost every time."[4] On the other hand, if you have strong views on a topic and are not interested in collaboration, tell the people what you want to do and get on with it [Chapter 8].

12. **Maintaining a collaborative climate in a team session initially rests with the primary facilitator, but overall is a shared responsibility.** Members in a group session take their behavioral conduct cues from the leader. One person, however, cannot sustain collaboration alone. As primary facilitator, you have every right to expect all others to follow your lead and share responsibility for maintaining it. If this is not understood by all, you need to explicitly state it [Chapter 8].

13. **Set a groundrule that handling disruptive behavior is always a responsibility shared by everyone present.** Each person shares responsibility with all others present to not be disruptive in the first place.

And, if someone is disruptive, in the spirit of secondary facilitation, any member present must feel free to confront the disrupter. The primary facilitator is never the sole facilitator of disruptive behavior [Chapter 8].

14. **Encourage constructive conflict; facilitate against destructive conflict.** Constructive conflict is a normal, healthy, occurrence in teams. It is the key to a team's critical thinking; encourage it. Destructive conflict can destroy a group beyond repair. Facilitate against it as soon as the signs of destruction begin to appear [Chapter 8].

These 14 principles are the core of "how to cash in on the collaborative brain power of a group." The detailed methods and the related sub-principles for doing it, of course, make up the content of this book. To me, the most rewarding aspect of these principles is that they were distilled from a wide variety of techniques, over many years, by interacting with thousands of practitioners, in many different organizational environments and settings.

To see a number of these principles in action, and to help teach others on your team how to practice them, I would highly recommend a 25-minute video entitled: *Mining Group Gold: The Quality Approach to Group Interaction.*[5]

The power of the video comes from our choice to shoot it as a documentary. Except for two short scenes done by professional actors, we simply filmed several work groups as they conducted a live, completely unrehearsed, team session "mining their group gold."

MINING GROUP GOLD IS A BOOK ABOUT LEADERSHIP

Back in 1984 when I wrote the original Xerox handbook, my focus was on how to run a quality meeting. However, as my knowledge and experience from using the handbook began to grow, it became clear that I was into something deeper and more complex. I was into the specifics of helping managers learn a whole new way of behaving and managing their work teams. My thrust was to provide the framework and alternative behaviors for changing one's leadership style from "manager as commander-and-controller" to one of "manager as facilitator." Much of what was learned from that whole effort shaped the content of the first edition of this book.

Now, in the second edition, with the collaboration principles articulated and the other chapter revisions made, *Mining Group Gold* becomes an even stronger book on leadership. Also, as more and more people at all levels in a particular organization are rewarded for living the behaviors and using the tools and processes advocated here, a marked cultural change to a collaborative organization will transpire.

Warren Bennis, Distinguished Professor of Business Administration at the University of Southern California, consultant, and noted author on leadership, was asked in an interview: *What are some of the traits you've found in leaders?"*

[Leaders] encourage healthy dissent. They surround themselves with people who are brave enough to say no. They know how to unleash others' talents. They pull rather than push people. They attract and energize others with their vision. They are able to clearly articulate the ideals toward which their organization should strive. And they are not afraid to change.

Bureaucracies have had their day. And that is what makes leaders so important. We need people with vision, who recognize the contributions of others, to lead our organizations, not bean counters, paper pushers, or micro-managers. Tomorrow's successful businesses will have torn down their hierarchical structures and become fluid, interactive, interdependent communities of collaborative colleagues.[6]

Ken Blanchard, president of Blanchard Associates and author of the mega-seller *The One Minute Manager*, in an interview with the American Society for Training and Development, was asked: *Over the past decade, what has changed most about the job of managing?"*

The role of managing has made a dramatic shift. In the past the emphasis was more on the manager as "boss." Today, managers must be partners with their people; the hierarchy is no longer where the action is. . . A Situational Leader . . . facilitates a partnering for performance process in which employees are treated more as colleagues, developing and implementing a plan of action together.

Everything in the field of management is now geared to move managers away from the "command-and-control" roles of judging and evaluating, to the post-industrial roles of supporting, encouraging, coaching and cheerleading. The most absurd thing managers can do today is act like they have all the answers. The world is changing too rapidly for that kind of arrogance . . . Only by collaborating with the people around you—direct reports, colleagues, customers, suppliers, and your boss—can you be an effective manager. While results are still important, how managers get those results has changed.[7]

In combination, the comments by Bennis and Blanchard neatly summarize the entire philosophical foundation upon which *Mining Group Gold* is built. Everything in this book is aimed at providing you with the specific behaviors, processes, and techniques to translate this philosophy into the realities of facilitative, collaborative leadership.

LOOKING AHEAD

In my second book, *Building Team Power: How to Unleash the Collaborative Genius of Work Teams,* (Irwin Professional Publishing, Burr Ridge, IL 1994), I use the first chapter to clearly demonstrate that the command-and-control bureaucracy is an outmoded architecture for the 90s and beyond. Bennis and Blanchard both stated this same belief in their earlier comments. The evidence in irrefutable. Organizations around the world are becoming bureaucracy busters because today's complex, competitive, turbulent, global marketplace demands it.

Tim Beran's description of American Yard Products' transformation to a team-based structure is typical of the changes taking place.

> By focusing our efforts around our core processes versus the old "command-and-control" departmental structure, we were able to break down functional cylinder barriers, allow more people to participate in improvement, raise the feeling among our employees of shared ownership in the company, and ultimately increase the rate of improvement of our business.
>
> We began restructuring by selecting and structuring a "Business Team" consisting of key leadership people. Using process mapping, we identified and accented our value-added business processes. Next, we distinguished tasks and activities within those processes and created teams from different departments to run them. By doing this, the paradigms of the traditional functional roles were crushed. The change in traditional roles and the creation of teams that own whole processes—as well as the results from the processes—has allowed a healthy company to become stronger.[8]

As you review the mechanics of the organizational transformation at American Yard Products, it is easy to see that teamwork and collaboration were at the root of planning and implementing the change, and at the core of making the new culture a success.

In a look at the strengths and weaknesses of business teams, Brian Dumaine notes:

> When teams work, there is nothing like them for turbocharging productivity. Beguiling examples abound: Scores of service companies like Federal Express and IDS have boosted productivity up to 40 percent by adopting self-managed work teams; Nynex is using teams to make the difficult transition from bureaucratic Baby Bell to a high-speed cruiser on the I-way; Boeing used teams to cut the number of engineering hang-ups

on its new 777 passenger jet by more than half. Says Boeing President Philip Condit: "Your competitiveness is your ability to use the skills and knowledge of your people most effectively, and teams are the best way to do that."

Yes, teams have troubles. They consume gallons of sweat and discouragement before yielding a penny of benefit. Companies make the investment only because they've realized that in a fast-moving, brutally competitive economy, the only sure thing harder than operating with teams is operating without them.[9]

Finally, technology's role in enhancing group collaboration no longer can be discounted. However, organized learning on how to gain the greatest collaborative benefits from the use of groupware products is still emerging. Chapter 9 directly addresses this critical problem by showing you how to integrate the principles of mining group gold into sessions using face-to-face groupware technology.

In envisioning the future, all I can see is unrelenting pressure on companies and governments around the world demanding that they figure out how to continuously leverage the synergy and collaborative brain power of all their employees in many configurations, at all levels, and across all functions in order to better satisfy their customers! It is the same vision I had in 1983, except now it is crystal clear and more vivid than ever. If you can't or won't do this, you'll be dead in the water. If you have the desire to make teamwork and collaboration a way of life in your organization, *Mining Group Gold* is your fundamental resource.

Notes Worksheet: DEVELOP WRITTEN RESPONSES TO THE TWO
ITEMS LISTED BELOW

What do you feel are the main learning points from Chapter 1?	Elaborate on why you feel these points are key.

Notes

1. D. T. Kearns and D. A. Nadler, *Prophets in the Dark: How Xerox Reinvented Itself and Beat Back the Japanese* (New York: HarperCollins Publisher, Inc., 1992), pp. xiii–xvi.

2. From *The Best and the Brightest* by David Halberstam, pp. 288–289. Copyright 1969, 1971, 1972 by David Halberstam. Reprinted by permission of Random House, Inc.

3. From *The Best and the Brightest* by David Halberstam, pp. 625–626. Copyright 1969, 1971, 1972 by David Halberstam. Reprinted by permission of Random House, Inc.

4. L. D. Eigen and J. P. Siegel, *The Manager's Book of Quotations* (New York: Amacom, 1989), p. 262.

5. CRM Films, Carlsbad, CA, © 1992, 1-800-421-0833.

6. The Association for Innovation in Management, "Executive Edge Interviews Warren Bennis: How to Develop Your Leadership Skills," *Executive Edge Newsletter*, June 1994, pp. 1, 3.

7. K. Blanchard, "An Interview with Kenneth Blanchard," Handout at the 50th ASTD International Conference, Anaheim, CA, May 19, 1994.

8. T. Beran, "How a Traditional Manufacturer Has Reorganized By Process," From speech presented at Clemson University's Third Annual Conference of the Alliance for P.E.O.P.L.E., San Diego, CA, May 24, 1994.

9. B. Dumaine, "The Trouble with Teams," *Fortune,* September 5, 1994, pp. 86, 92.

CHAPTER TWO

MISMANAGING GROUP GOLD: HIGH COSTS, LITTLE GOLD

CHAPTER OBJECTIVES

➤ To set the stage for the rest of the book.

➤ To document the high cost of meetings in terms of time and money.

➤ To establish the leverage ratio as the way to strategically think about meeting costs.

INTRODUCTION

Meetings, bloody meetings. For most managers, they start early on Monday and go on and on and on throughout the week. There even is an old cliché that defines a manager as a person either coming from, going to, or sitting in a meeting.

In the modern organization, where collaboration and inter-dependence are inescapable requirements for success, group sessions are a fact of life. Today, more than ever, meetings have become the forum for sharing, sorting, processing, regrouping, and distributing data and information.

In view of their role as the backbone of an organization, it is tragic that most meetings are so poorly conceived and poorly conducted. The "gold mine" of ideas, information, data, knowledge, and creativity that participants bring to group sessions is being misunderstood, put down, ignored, or even worse, left buried in the minds of the participants.

The liabilities of shoddy meetings are legendary: too much talking and not enough listening; too much assuming and not enough understanding; too much attacking and not enough crediting; too much taking and not enough giving; too much storming and not enough performing; too many people and not enough room; too many topics and not enough time. The list could go on but the point is made.

In fact, it is the negative aspects of group sessions, or as Luke Skywalker might describe it, "the dark side of the force," that gives rise to the caustic jokes about meetings. While the jokes and quips may be funny, they strike close to the truth. Here are some of my favorites.

"A meeting is a gathering where people speak up, say nothing, then all disagree."

"A meeting is a place where you keep the minutes but throw away the hours."

"A meeting is an interaction where the unwilling, selected from the uninformed, led by the unsuitable, to discuss the unnecessary, are required to write a report on the unimportant."

"A meeting is indispensable when you don't want to accomplish anything."

"The best meeting is a group of three with one person sick and another out of town."

"A faculty meeting can be described as a bunch of screaming anarchists tied together by a common parking lot."

Will Rogers, invited to sit in on a committee meeting of an organization that ordinarily did not permit the presence of outsiders, remarked when the meeting was over, "I agreed to repeat nothing and I'll keep my promise. But I gotta admit, I heard nothing worth repeating."

The thing that is most disturbing about group sessions is the lack of effort by most group leaders to do anything about how meetings are planned and conducted. We know there are problems with a significant percentage of the group sessions we attend or lead, but we have come to accept mediocrity as the norm. Why? Perhaps this debilitating condition has been created in many organizations by a phenomenon best defined by a Chinese proverb that says, "To the mediocre, mediocrity appears great."

In any event, inefficient, ineffective, and unproductive meetings are tolerated within educational institutions, business enterprises, government agencies, hospitals, and voluntary associations as an everyday cost of doing business much like leasing office space and paying taxes is an everyday cost. However, while these organizations are continually looking to obtain the most favorable lease arrangements and are constantly searching for loopholes to cut their taxes, these same organizations virtually ignore the tremendous cost of execrable meetings. Mosvick and Nelson reinforce this point quite passionately:

> Ineffective meeting management is fast becoming a national disgrace. Poorly planned and poorly run meetings are the worst kept secret of America's vaunted business skills. In competitive challenges at home and abroad they are our Achilles' heel. Contemporary business is a hotly contested race which requires that every component of our competitive position be examined. Yet few companies have even begun to take a serious look at the largest remaining item of containable costs in most organizations.[1]

Poorly conceived and conducted meetings do not have to be passively accepted as a way of life within today's organizations. You and others like yourself can make a difference—

you can learn how to be "a miner of group gold." This book will show you how to open the treasure chest of knowledge and information buried in the heads of meeting attendees and get these nuggets of wisdom shared and processed into outputs that satisfy everyone.

In order to mine group gold successfully, you'll need to master a few simple tools and techniques. What these are and how they serve to improve the productivity of group sessions is the subject of this book.

COSTS OF GROUP SESSIONS

Figures can be misleading; we've all heard about the man who drowned wading across a lake with an average depth of three feet. This section is not intended to mislead you or overwhelm you with numbers. It is intended to underscore the terribly high costs of bringing three or more people together inside the four walls of a conference room to share and process information.

Every time you get up from your desk to attend another meeting, your actions are sending a powerful message. They are saying quite clearly: "This meeting is so important that I am willing to set aside everything else that I could be doing to join with the other attendees." The costs to you and your meeting partners, and in turn to the organization, are much higher than you might imagine.

Think of it this way. If eight people each spend half an hour preparing for a two-hour meeting that wastes everyone's time, that's a total of twenty work hours lost: four work hours in preparation time (eight people times half an hour each) plus sixteen work hours in meeting time (eight people times two hours each). Those hours come "right out of the hides" of the participants. Add another hour of secretarial support time that the meeting caller required for tasks like scheduling, typing, phoning, copying, etc., and you are up to a total of twenty-one direct work hours wasted on one two-hour session.

But that's not the end of the calculations. There is another associated cost: lost opportunity. Collectively, the eight meeting participants and the secretary have lost the opportunity to apply those same twenty-one work hours to more productive tasks. Now, if we take the twenty-one direct-time work hours, plus the twenty-one work hours of lost opportunity, our seemingly routine two-hour session with eight people ends up carrying a price tag of forty-two squandered work hours!

There is no such thing as a free meeting. Each time you decide to call a meeting of your own, or decide to attend someone else's, you are not making a trivial decision. From a monetary standpoint, the direct costs of poorly spent meeting time is staggering. A 1989 study of 2,000 business leaders by Harrison Conference Centers and Hofstra University reveals that unproductive meeting time has a direct cost to American business of more than $37 billion a year.[2] Mosvick and Nelson state that one carefully costed-out analysis of a mid-sized Fortune 500 company yielded a conservative estimate that this business lost $71 million a year because of poor meeting management.[3]

The ease with which time and money can be unproductively frittered away is exemplified by the following anecdote from *The Wall Street Journal.*

Robert Lefton, president of Psychological Associates Inc., a St. Louis consulting firm, recently attended a meeting at a large West Coast manufacturing company that had been scheduled to consider a major restructuring. Instead, the 18 executives present lapsed into a 90-minute discussion about what food to serve at an office party. "I asked the guy sitting next to me to estimate the salaries of the people in the room; he figured out that the conversation cost the company $2,200," Lefton says.[4]

In a 1995 update to my original (1989) study to determine the cost of the average meeting within the 24,000-person Development and Manufacturing Group of Xerox, I discovered that:

1. The average meeting was comprised of seven people organizationally equivalent to four senior engineers, two project managers, and one second-level manager.

2. The average length of the session was 60 minutes.

3. Accounting for fully loaded salaries (to reflect payroll taxes, benefits, general overhead, support help, etc.), the cost was $427.[5]

When that amount is multiplied by 4,500 meetings per week (the same as in 1989, but still a conservative number for an international organization the size and complexity of D&M), and then by 52 to convert to an annualized cost, the final result is an attention grabbing *$100.4 million in real meeting costs.* This is a $22.3 million dollar increase (28.5 percent) over the results from six years earlier.

Recapturing just 15 to 20 percent of that admittedly conservative cost figure through improved meeting performance, still translates into substantial savings of $15.1 to 20.1 million for D&M.

Exhibit 2–1, a chart developed by the 3M Meeting Management Team, can serve as a mechanism for quickly calculating a meeting's fully loaded direct costs.[6] To use Exhibit 2–1, just add up the salary figures for all persons present. The total will be the per-hour cost of the meeting.

For example, if two individuals in the $40,000 bracket and two in the $30,000 bracket meet for one hour, the cost to the company is $134 ($77 + $57). When the meeting extends to two hours the cost is $268. If a company averages 10 two-hour meetings like this each week, the real dollar cost for one year is $139,360.

So far, we have been dealing with direct meeting costs. Often overlooked are the indirect costs—the ripple effect that poor meetings have as their negative consequences spread beyond the meeting room to encroach on other parts of the organization. Doyle and Straus explain.

Exhibit 2-1: COST OF MEETINGS TO NEAREST DOLLAR PER HOUR

Annual Salary	Number of Participants									
	10	9	8	7	6	5	4	3	2	1
$50,000	$481	$433	$385	$337	$288	$240	$192	$144	$96	$48
40,000	385	346	308	269	231	192	154	115	77	38
30,000	288	260	231	202	173	144	115	87	57	28
25,000	240	216	192	168	144	120	96	72	48	24
20,000	192	173	154	135	115	96	77	58	38	19

Reprinted from *How to Run Better Meetings* by permission of McGraw-Hill, Inc.

When a meeting blows up, when nothing get accomplished or people become frustrated and angry, the participants take their frustrations back with them to their jobs or homes. Not only do participants of the meeting waste time cooling off, but they waste other people's time griping about what happened. These are some of the hidden costs of unsuccessful meetings. Harold Reimer, a researcher in the field, estimates that the cost of time lost after ineffective meetings amounts to $800,000 per year for every 1,000 employees. We call this the "meeting recovery syndrome."[7]

Time and money, money and time, with respect to meetings they intertwine. And, when all the costs are added up, it blows your mind.

THE LEVERAGE RATIO

It's hard to pick up the financial pages of any newspaper today without finding another story on a leveraged buyout. A group of eight or ten investors with $85 million can buy a $1 billion company. On a more personal level, if you have ever put 20 percent down on a $100,000 home or put $1,200 down on a $15,000 automobile, you have leveraged your money. You have invested a small amount of your own money and gained control of an asset worth ten, fifteen, or twenty times your investment. Utilizing small, up-front cash investments that yield high returns is leveraging.

This concept also applies to meeting improvement, and it must be understood in any organization seriously bent on salvaging some of the time and money being squandered on wasteful, unproductive meetings. Let's use a little vignette to illustrate the power of the leverage ratio in recouping wasted meeting dollars.

Cynthia's Session

Cynthia, a manager, calls a meeting of herself and nine other people in her department. Cynthia has not read *Mining Group*

Gold, nor has she had any training in the tools and processes of good meeting management. She does not take time to plan the structure and process of this session. She is too busy with other, more important, tasks. Instead, Cynthia goes in, as she often does, and "wings it."

The meeting is scheduled to run from 1:00 to 4:00 P.M. The first 15 minutes is taken up arguing over "why are we here?" and "what do we want to achieve by the end of this meeting?" Another 20 minutes is spent pounding out an agenda. Facilitating the side conversations and personal attacks between Sam and Mary, who have no interest in the meeting's subject matter, requires 10 more minutes. Another 5 minutes is consumed arguing over whether or not George should be present to provide his insights on the topic. A vote reveals a majority of the group wants George to be there. Then, because the session is interrupted searching for George, getting him to the session, and bringing him up to date, another 10 minutes is lost. Twelve minutes is lost backtracking over data and decisions because no one is recording and posting this information as it comes up. Mark requires 18 minutes of special facilitation to keep him focused. His only interest is how the project will be implemented, and he keeps bringing up numerous issues that are out of place for this strategic-level discussion.

The whole group eventually shares and processes the appropriate information. They reach a consensus on the issue under discussion and the session adjourns at 4 P.M. Was this a productive session? Cynthia thinks so, and the other attendees feel the same way. They finished on time. They worked through a tough issue and reached consensus on how they wanted to proceed. Three hours to reach consensus on a sensitive issue—"hey, not bad."

Let's review this episode from a different perspective. One hour and 30 minutes of the three hours was consumed by disruptive activities that could have been prevented or reduced through proper planning of the meeting's structure and process and through better meeting leadership skills. For the purpose of this illustration, let's say that up-front planning and better in-session facilitation could have eliminated the 1½ hours of the misused time. We now can demonstrate the power of the leverage ratio.

Leverage Ratio Calculations

Let's say that Cynthia has read *Mining Group Gold* and is familiar with the tools and processes advocated here (especially the leverage ratio). Therefore, instead of being too busy to plan, Cynthia invests one hour of her most precious resource, her personal time, in planning the structure and process of her upcoming session. The session achieves its desired outcomes in 1½ hours instead of three. Her planning and in-session meeting management skills have cut the meeting time by 50 percent through improved session productivity.

With 10 people at the group session (Cynthia plus nine others), each person is given a gift of time of 1½ hours. For the whole group, that translates into 15 work hours saved. Fifteen work hours saved for a one hour investment is a *15:1 leverage ratio!* Ten people are released to go back to their jobs. They can perform 10 other tasks that would otherwise have had to wait while the group unproductively "burned" that same period of time. Also not to be overlooked, Cynthia's personal investment of one hour is returned to her 150 percent. Exhibit 2–2 shows calculations for figuring the monetary value of the leverage ratio.

No matter how you look at it, the leverage ratio is a critical meeting concept. It clearly demonstrates how small investments in advanced planning and the acquisition of meeting leadership skills is returned to the organization many times over.

Exhibit 2–2: LEVERAGE RATIO RETURN ON INVESTMENT

Participant	Salary	Hourly Cost from Exhibit 2–1
Cynthia	$50,000	$ 48
Average for other participants	40,000	346
		$ 394 Cost/hour for the session

Return: 1.5 hours saved x $394 = $591

Investment: Up-front preparation time; 1 hour @ $48

$591 returned on an investment of $48 is slightly over a 12:1 Return on Investment.

All of these savings do not neatly and cleanly flow to the bottom line, of course. What these savings do is translate into increased productivity—more and better work for the same dollars. They surface as increased time for people to learn new skills in areas critical to the organization. They show up as expanded work capability—people have more time to take on more tasks and wider responsibilities.

For many organizations, recovering just a fraction of the time and money being blown on poorly planned and facilitated group sessions could mean the difference between being able to ignite a vigorous climate of growth and prosperity or being forced to struggle for mere survival.

MEETINGS: A FORUM FOR LEADERSHIP AND RUNNING THE BUSINESS

In spite of all the drawbacks and expenses associated with bringing people together, one fact remains: Group sessions are the lifeblood of organizations. Whether we like it or not, sitting down face to face with a group of people often is the right way—the ONLY way—to process information and achieve goals. Meetings are the essential medium of managerial work. Kieffer has put it as succinctly as anyone.

> Meetings are the fulcrum for all commercial and non-commercial transactions, the central nervous system of an information society, the center stage for personal performance. . . . [O]nce you perceive that meetings are perhaps the single most important "window" on business and professional life, the window through which we see and evaluate and are seen and evaluated, you will be far less casual about invitations to meet and far more demanding of the meetings you choose to call or attend.
>
> General judgments about you will inevitably be made because how you handle a meeting reveals how you might handle a future job necessarily full of meetings. There are few visible bases on which to make judgments regarding managerial and leadership skills, and the

ability to manage meetings is as accurate a reflection of such skills as one can find.[8]

Green and Lazarus, documenting findings based on survey results of over 1,000 executives from a wide range of functions, including general management, sales, marketing, finance, manufacturing, and human resources, fully substantiate the perspective laid down by Kieffer.

Make no mistake about it, meetings are management. Or stated more accurately, meetings are a microcosm of management. Better meetings are inextricably linked to better management.

One of the survey's most important findings is that, in terms of human resources and the development of management potential, business people do indeed see meetings as management. And how well [people] manage and participate in business meetings can play a crucial role in how fast they climb the corporate ladder. The study revealed that executives who run meetings well are perceived to be better managers by both their superiors and their peers. Conversely, those who fail to run meetings effectively are often considered to be lacking in critical management skills. Statistically, 87 percent of those surveyed found that a person's ability to lead meetings affects people's perceptions of their management ability.

[Regarding participation in sessions] 81 percent of the respondents said that their perception of a participant's ability is definitely affected by the quality of his or her participation in a meeting. . . . [O]ne thing seems perfectly clear: an individual's performance in meetings is a key to promotability. Those people who most effectively participate in, and manage, meetings are most likely to head the companies of the future.[9]

In today's competitive, turbulent, complex, interdependent economic environment, teams, teamwork, and collaboration, by necessity, are the heart and soul of world class organizations for the 90s and beyond. Teams have two assets that exceed those of any individual on the team: they possess more knowledge, and they can think in a greater variety of ways. These potential assets may not always be reached however. Because of poor facilitation and leadership, teams may fall into so much dysfunctional conflict that they cannot operate. On the other hand, excellent facilitation and leadership can move the team to realize its full potential and produce a superior output which propels everyone's commitment and feelings of satisfaction to their zenith.

Group sessions are not to be trifled with. Your organization's success, and your own personal growth, development, and promotability, depends on your ability to seize every meeting opportunity as a forum for role-modeling facilitation and collaborative leadership.

In order to achieve this "best case" result, certain tools, techniques, and processes must be learned and routinely practiced by managers and non-managers at all levels of your organization. What these tools, techniques, and processes are, and how they can increase the value and productivity of your company's group sessions, constitutes the remainder of this book.

Notes Worksheet: DEVELOP WRITTEN RESPONSES TO THE TWO
ITEMS LISTED BELOW

What do you feel are the main learning points from Chapter 2?	Elaborate on why you feel these points are key.

Notes

1. R. K. Mosvick and R. B. Nelson, *We've Got to Start Meeting Like This* (Glenview, IL: Scott Foresman and Company, 1987), pp. 4–5.

2. "Study Says Meetings Waste Precious Time," *The Cleveland Plain Dealer*, March 31, 1989, p. 15C.

3. Mosvick and Nelson, *Meeting Like This*, p. 4.

4. C. Hymowitz, "A Survival Guide to the Office Meeting," *The Wall Street Journal*, June 21, 1988, p. 41.

5. See: The 3M Meeting Management Team, *How to Run Better Business Meetings*, (New York: McGraw-Hill, 1987). This group has developed a rule of thumb to estimate the fully loaded per-hour cost of a meeting: Double the value of the base pay of each participant. As they aptly point out on page 7: "If five people meet for an hour, and each makes $40,000 per year, their salaries for that hour total $96. Base salary, however, is only part of the story. To it must be added payroll taxes, fringe benefits, and general overhead. Consideration must be given to secretarial and preparation time. By doubling the base of the participants, these expenses are roughly accounted for."

6. 3M Management Team, *Better Business Meetings*, p. 14.

7. M. Doyle and D. Straus, *How to Make Meetings Work*, (New York: The Berkley Publishing Group, 1976), pp. 8–9.

8. G. D. Kieffer, *The Strategy of Meetings*, (New York: Simon and Schuster, 1988), pp. 12–13, 20.

9. W. A. Green and H. Lazarus, "Are Today's Executives Meeting with Success?", *Journal of Management Development*, vol. 10, no. 1, 1991, pp. 22–23.

CHAPTER THREE

THE KEY TO THE GOLD MINE: FACILITATION

CHAPTER OBJECTIVES

➤ To define the role and fundamental behaviors of a facilitator.

➤ To show that the manager, administrator, or chairperson as a practicing facilitator is an organizational requirement for the 1990s and beyond.

➤ To show how facilitation activities complement and strengthen the manager's role.

INTRODUCTION

The leadership approach advocated throughout this book is one of facilitation. As the chapter title suggests, facilitation is the key to unlocking the gold mine of wisdom and knowledge buried in the heads of your people. When released, this wisdom can be used to solve problems, make decisions, resolve conflicts, develop alternatives, create strategies, heal interpersonal strife, and much, much more. The family group manager,[1] the administrator, the school principal, the committee chairperson, the supervisor, the team leader—anyone managing a meeting in order to cash in on the collaborative brain power of a group—will be practicing the same set of skills: facilitation skills.

What happens without facilitation? The following incident will give you an idea.

The sixth-grade safety patrol boy limped into the school principal's office with a black eye and a bruised knot on his forehead. The principal asked, "Arnie, what on earth happened to you?"

Arnie replied, "I tried to help a little old lady across the busy street in front of our school."

The principal, in a voice filled with disbelief, responded, "Oh come now, you didn't get beaten up because you tried to help an old lady across the street!"

Arnie exclaimed, "Oh yes I did. She didn't want to go!"

Force, power, authority, resistance, no commitment to the final destination, lack of mutual understanding about the situation, ill will between people, bruises . . . all of these elements are found in this little story.

These same elements, plus many others, are found in thousands and thousands of meetings across America each day where everyone is doing battle over content and no one is paying attention to facilitation—to *group process.*

Even though the little old lady met her desired outcome of not going across the street, the wasteful, dysfunctional, energy-consuming process that transpired extracted a heavy toll on both parties. Facilitation of this encounter could have led to a much more productive outcome.

Keep this episode in mind. After reading this book, come back to it and determine how you would have facilitated the situation if you had stumbled on these two people at the beginning of their interaction. Since facilitation is the key to the gold mine, let's start by defining the role of the facilitator.

WHAT IS A FACILITATOR?

Very simply, a facilitator is a person who helps a group free itself from internal obstacles or difficulties so that it may more efficiently and effectively pursue the achievement of its desired outcomes for a given meeting. Lao-Tse, one of the great Chinese philosophers who lived under the Chou dynasty, developed a superb definition of a facilitator over 2,400 years ago when he said, "A good leader is best when people barely know that he leads. A good leader talks little but when the work is done, the aim fulfilled, all others will say, 'We did this ourselves.'"

Elaborating on the wisdom of Lao-Tse, Bob Kelsch, an organization effectiveness specialist formerly on my staff, describes the facilitator's role.

> In the purest sense, when wearing the 'facilitator's hat' an individual acts as a neutral servant of the people. By that I mean the person focuses on guiding without directing; bringing about action without disruption; helping people self-discover new approaches and solutions to problems; knocking down walls which have been built between people while preserving structures of value; and, above all, appreciating people as people. All of this must be done without leaving any fingerprints.[2]

Effective facilitation is at the core of team-based organizations emphasizing collaborative approaches to problem solving, planning, and decision making. As more and more managers come to understand what facilitation means, internalize the philosophy, and practice the fundamental behaviors in a quality way, the payoff will be significant in terms of enhanced team productivity.

THE MANAGER AS FACILITATOR

There is little doubt that managers are facing the challenge of their professional lives. Downsizing, restructuring, redistricting, mergers, acquisitions, and consolidations are responses to fierce global competition. Additionally, an unrelenting need to improve customer satisfaction, product quality, and level of service are pressing managers into more demanding, more facilitative roles. They are being asked to take on more responsibilities in flatter organizational structures, which places them closer to problems they often don't have the necessary technical expertise to deal with.

Managers are being asked to do more with less. Learning and practicing facilitation skills will be the surest way for managers to provide the new level of leadership required to meet these challenges, and this is true regardless of industry or professional occupation.

Although the emphasis of this section is on the manager and on the heavy facilitation requirements that will be placed on the expanded managerial role throughout the 90s and into the twenty-first century, much of what is said here also rings true for school and hospital administrators, committee chairpersons, task-force leaders, agency heads, and the like.

The need for people to acquire facilitation skills is well-articulated by Naisbitt and Aburdene in their national bestseller, *Re-inventing the Corporation*.

> In the re-invented corporation, we are shifting from manager as order-giver to manager as facilitator. We used to think that the manager's job was to know all the answers. But [today and in the future], the new manager ought, rather, to know the questions, to be concerned about them and involve others in finding the answers. Today's manager needs to be more of a facilitator— someone skilled in eliciting answers from others, perhaps from people who do not even know that they know. The most successful companies of the new information era are committed to the manager's new role as developer and cultivator of human potential.[3]

Building facilitation capabilities throughout all levels of an organization's hierarchy is not some passing fad. It is a necessary, ongoing effort driven by the need to continually respond to the question, "What must we do to meet customer requirements faster, cheaper, and better than any of our competitors?"

Organizations insisting that the knowledge and practice of facilitation behaviors permeate all levels of their hierarchy will be the ones leading the race into the twenty-first century. Why? Because they will be "mining their group gold" and using it as an asset in the formulation of strategies, plans, decisions, and solutions to provide a level of customer satisfaction beyond the reach of their competition.

Edgar Schein, a consultant to many Fortune 500 companies and the Sloan Fellows Professor of Management at M.I.T., also strengthens the case for the manager as facilitator with his argument that *effective managers are helpers*. They make certain that subordinates, peers, and supervisors get the help they need in order to get things done, to succeed, and to achieve their goals.

> As for general managers, whose responsibilities cut across various business functions and who manage complete organizational units, in many functions the subordinates are often each more expert than their boss. It is in such situations, where the boss's job is to integrate, coordinate, and blend the expertise of others for coherent decisions, that the skills of helping become most relevant.
>
> In a technologically complex society neither managers nor consultants can really give commands or tell others what to do. Even in medicine, specialists and surgeons are finding themselves in complex relationships with their patients where they are helping those patients to make a beneficial decision rather than just "ordering" a given procedure.[4]

In an article based on research conducted under a two-year joint project between the American Society for Training and Development and the United States Department of Labor, Carnevale augments the picture being sketched by the others.

> In the new workplace, both autonomy and the managerial function have been pushed down the line, challenging top-down management practices and the hierarchies that housed them. In the new organization, authority, responsibility, and resources will be drawn down the line toward the point of production and service delivery. . . . New technologies and a greater reliance on working teams at the point of production and service delivery

have made the working team more autonomous. The supervisor has had to assume a less aggressive role in managing work processes and a more supportive role in facilitating the work of front line teams.[5]

Finally, to avoid the impression that business and industry are the only sectors where a significant increase in the demand for facilitation expertise is taking place, a word about school-based (or site-based) management will show that the same requirement, possibly on an even grander scale, is occurring within our educational system.

Although school-based management takes many forms, the goal is to empower school staff by providing authority, flexibility, and resources to solve the educational problems particular to their schools.

Principals are required to chair each school's planning team, typically a group of students, teachers, parents, and sometimes other community members. Day-to-day operations of the school building and general administration of the school staff remains the responsibility of the principal. But the planning team now can have a great deal of influence over many of the long-range issues affecting student performance, including the curriculum, teaching methods, and school environment.

Principals in particular, but all other members of the school-based management team as well, must become adept at facilitation. It is mandatory if school-based planning is to succeed.

David examines the rationale for the school-based approach and the necessity for decentralized, collaborative decision making.

The rationale for school-based management rests on two well-established propositions:

The school is the primary decision-making unit; and, its corollary, decisions should be made at the lowest possible level.

Change requires ownership that comes from the opportunity to participate in defining change and the flexibility to adapt it to individual circumstances; the corollary is that change does not result from externally imposed procedures.

39

In practice, these propositions translate into two policies that define the essence of school-based management: (1) increasing school autonomy through some combination of site budgetary control and relief from constraining rules and regulations; and, (2) sharing the authority to make decisions with teachers, parents, students, and sometimes other community members.[6]

The direction described by these experts accentuates group-oriented, facilitative leadership behaviors. Increased delegation, shared decision making, empowerment, and management of cross-functional teams is not based on an autocratic model of *control*. It is grounded in an open, collaborative, concept of *teamwork*.

Facilitation is a necessity for the 1990s and beyond; it is the road over which successful organizations will ride!

FUNDAMENTAL BEHAVIORS OF THE FACILITATOR

Behavioral science literature is clear regarding the typical behaviors to be role-modeled by the manager, task force chairperson, administrator, team leader or other person acting as facilitator. Likert[7] first described these behaviors in the early 1960s, but it took until the mid-80s for American business, educational, and governmental organizations to begin to embrace them widely. A facilitator, no matter what his or her other title may be, behaves in the following ways:

➤ Focuses the energies of the group on defining and accomplishing common desired outcomes.

➤ Helps the group use efficient communication processes that provide better information, more technical knowledge, more facts, and more experience for decision-making purposes than the leader working alone could marshal.

➤ Uses group decision making at every appropriate opportunity to earn each member's support for the final decision, thus gaining members' commitment to execute it fully.

➤ Knows that at times decisions must be made rapidly and cannot wait for group processes; therefore, anticipates these emergencies and establishes procedures with the group for handling them so that action can be taken rapidly with group support.

➤ Takes primary responsibility for establishing and maintaining a thoroughly supportive atmosphere throughout the group; encourages every member to participate.

➤ Strengthens the group and its processes by being careful to see that all matters that involve and affect the group are dealt with by the group, while at the same time avoiding those items or tasks that do not concern the group. (These items are handled by appropriate subgroups or individuals who give feedback on progress and results to the whole group.)

➤ Fosters self-discovery of alternatives and solutions by protecting group members and their ideas from attack, so members feel secure in sharing and exploring a multitude of proposals, ideas, thoughts, and opinions.

In order to have the fullest impact on organizational success, the facilitation philosophy and behaviors have to be a shared value among a majority of the line managers and administrators in an organization. The facilitation role must not evolve into the exclusive domain of a few staff people on whom the line groups depend for their facilitation services.

Even if facilitation experts exist in an organization, they will comprise a very lean staff. One person for every 3,000 to 5,000 employees is a common ratio. With such small staffs, the third-party facilitation help that does exist will be concentrated on a few highest-priority sessions. In most cases, work groups, task forces, and committees must learn to facilitate themselves. It is the only way they can count on day-to-day facilitation within their unit.

For the goal of self-facilitation to be realized, every manager needs to be at the forefront, learning and modeling the basic facilitation behaviors presented here and encouraging others on the team to follow his or her lead.

In the broadest sense, facilitation occurs any time any group member behaves in a manner that advances the group toward any of three basic goals:

1. Developing or refining a structure and/or process that promotes achievement of the work session's desired outcomes.

2. Making certain that information and data is shared, understood and processed in an open, collaborative environment.

3. Removing any internal blockages hindering the accomplishment of the session's desired outcomes.

Facilitation revolves around these three goals; every team member must understand them and be prepared to share the responsibility for achieving them.

FACILITATION IN CROSS-FUNCTIONAL TEAMS

Increasingly today, organizations of all types are using cross-functional teams to study problems and make joint decisions in areas that once were the exclusive domain of middle and upper management. Such teams are widely used in Continuous Quality Improvement (CQI) approaches. Because these teams are often self-formed and, as such, do not have a clear-cut, formally designated manager or leader, their long-term effectiveness can be at risk before they even get off the ground. In many CQI teams, the participants are close in rank and not in direct reporting relationships. These internal dynamics retard the team's ability to get moving as a collaborative team.

My experience indicates that the root cause is the lack of a catalyst—a team leader who also assumes the complementary role of primary facilitator. Too often excessive politeness rules. No one seems willing to step forward, to assume the mantle of leader/primary facilitator, and to orchestrate collaborative processes for fear of alienating all the others. As a consequence, when the team does meet, agendas are seldom focused to include everyone's needs, information processing easily gets sidetracked, confusion sets in, destructive conflict runs unabated, and action responsibilities are not completed because they were left vague. Team members soon dread going to team sessions—first they tune-out, then they drop-out. Over time, the team erodes and fails to meet its goals.

Cross-functional teams cannot perform without some member assuming the critical dual role of team leader/primary facilitator. The first meeting must be used to determine who, *initially*, will do this for what period of time. If the team can't come to a satisfactory decision by itself, then someone from management, who has a stake in the team's deliverables, will have to assign someone this role. After others have learned the primary facilitation behaviors from the team leader, the primary facilitator's role can begin to rotate, but under no circumstances should a cross-functional team meet without a designated primary facilitator for every session.

FACILITATION IS A SHARED RESPONSIBILITY

Although one person (the group manager, administrator, task force chairperson, or other designated individual) has the formal responsibility of being the primary facilitator for a particular session, facilitation must be shared by everyone in attendance. All other attendees are designated as secondary facilitators.

Whenever a group comes together to trade information, strategize, solve problems, or make decisions, every member of the group must share the responsibility for making the session as successful as it can possibly be. By recognizing that facilitation is a group function to which all members can contribute, the primary facilitator helps to develop a culture of teamwork and group cohesion. Developing a shared responsibility for facilitation ensures that all group resources will be used productively.

No one person can possibly be sensitive to all task, process, and individual problems existing at any given moment in a group session. Some members may be more skilled at using task-oriented behaviors such as proposing, seeking information, testing comprehension, and summarizing. Others may be more prone to concentrate on group-oriented behaviors such as encouraging, harmonizing, and performance checking. Some may be more adept at helping particular members understand how, perhaps unconsciously, they are side-tracking the group, while others may be more skillful at resolving conflict. Still others may be better able to write quickly and neatly on flip charts, and so on.

The key point is that the facilitation of a session is not the sole responsibility of the primary facilitator. That person should expect, and receive, facilitation assistance (i.e., secondary facilitation) from everyone in attendance if a session's productivity is to be maximized.

SWITCHING HATS

Initially, most people are not effective at being the primary facilitator and, at the same time, being a full participant in the ongoing content discussion. Experience has shown that more often than not, if the primary facilitator actively participates in the content of the meeting, he or she invariably gets swept up in the debate, discussion, analysis, disagreement, etc., and forgets about the facilitation. It is true that some people can do both jobs quite effectively; however, they are the exception rather than the rule.

If the manager, committee chairperson, or administrator is the primary facilitator for a group and, as is usually the case at first, is not able to move naturally between the dual roles of group facilitator and full group participant, then these roles need to be consciously split.

The reason for mentally separating the two roles is to emphasize and preserve the integrity of the facilitation process. By thinking in terms of "wearing two hats" and by switching them as required throughout the meeting, the primary facilitator will not forget about the facilitation role whenever he or she enters the discussion as a group participant.

As primary facilitator, the chief concern must be *facilitation* (helping the group free itself from internal obstacles or difficulties so that it can more efficiently and effectively pursue its desired outcomes) and not *content* (getting enmeshed in the task-related dialogue and activities).

Obviously, when facilitating your own group, you may want to contribute your perspectives and ideas to the ongoing dialogue and activities. When this occurs, you need to signal that you are stepping out of the facilitator role and into the role of group participant. Your inputs should be shared with the group and processed in line with the approach being utilized. When you are done, announce that you are returning to the primary facilitator role and proceed with assisting the group process until the next occasion arises where personal input is deemed appropriate. Here is an example:

> "For the moment, I'd like to slip on my manager's hat and provide my ideas on the bonus plan. First of all, . . ."

> "Those are the main thoughts I wanted to provide right now, especially the concept of a 10 percent initial buy-in for all eligible participants. Putting my facilitator's hat back on, I've noticed that Jack and Diane have been quiet throughout this discussion. What are your views on the bonus plan proposal?"

Please remember, being primary facilitator in no way removes you from participating in meeting content. However, it is imperative that you distinguish your facilitator role from your active group member (content) role each time these roles change during a group session. Also, from the group members' point of view, if it is not clear whether the primary facilitator is operating from the facilitation role or the active group member (content) role, secondary facilitation requires that the discussion be stopped momentarily to ask the primary facilitator, "I'm not certain which role you are operating from at this point. Would you please clarify which hat you are wearing?"

Granted, role-splitting by the facilitator is somewhat mechanical and artificial. However, this procedure does deliver a significant two-pronged payback. It ensures the integrity of the facilitation process, while at the same time it provides a means for the primary facilitator to actively furnish his or her personal inputs regarding the issues at hand.

YOU'RE ALWAYS IN CHARGE

From a managerial standpoint, being a miner of group gold does not diminish your assigned responsibilities, compromise your ability to make tough decisions, or weaken your ability to lead the group. Practicing the art of excellent facilitation is not being soft on your people; it is not "turning the candy store over to the kids." Practicing the art of excellent facilitation does require self-discipline and, in some situations, even requires behavioral or stylistic changes in the way you currently interact with the group.

Simply put, practicing the art of excellent facilitation never compromises your ability to manage the group. The underlying reason is that as the formal leader of the group, you always retain full responsibility for the group's performance and for seeing that the group meets the demands and expectations placed upon it by the larger organization.

Actually, having this full responsibility affords you the opportunity to decide to take advantage of the various facilitation behaviors described in this book in order to enhance your effectiveness in "managing with people."

A FINAL POINT

Once you begin to view each group session as a gold mine of ideas, thoughts, solutions, approaches, and insights; once you begin to see yourself as a "gold miner"—a facilitator—then your attitude toward group sessions will change forever. Productive meetings always will be within reach.

Using this orientation information as a foundation, the remaining chapters will highlight specific considerations, processes, and activities for enhancing your ability to plan and facilitate group sessions. In short, you will learn to be a "miner of group gold."

Notes Worksheet: DEVELOP WRITTEN RESPONSES TO THE TWO
ITEMS LISTED BELOW

What do you feel are the main learning points from Chapter 3?	Elaborate on why you feel these points are key.

Notes

1. The term *family group* is used in organizational development literature to designate any organizational group consisting of the formal head of that group plus all those who directly report to the formal head. This person is called the *family group manager*.

2. B. Kelsch, Personal communication.

3. J. Naisbitt and P. Aburdene, *Re-inventing the Corporation* (New York: Warner Books, 1985), pp. 52–53.

4. E. H. Schein, *Process Consultation: Lessons for Managers and Consultants*, vol. II (Reading, MA: Addison-Wesley, 1987), pp. 8–9.

5. A. P. Carnevale, "Managing Training Today and Tomorrow," *Training and Development Journal*, December 1988, pp. 20–21.

6. J. L. David, "Synthesis of Research on School-Based Management," *Educational Leadership* 46(8) (May 1989): p. 46.

7. R. Likert, *New Patterns of Management* (New York: McGraw-Hill, 1961), pp. 170–72.

CHAPTER FOUR

PLANNING THE STRUCTURE OF A SESSION TO MINE GROUP GOLD: FIVE STEPS TO SUCCESS

CHAPTER OBJECTIVES

➤ To provide pointers that will simplify the task of planning the structure of a group session.

➤ To present several guidesheets to assist in transferring these ideas into actions.

INTRODUCTION

Efficient and productive meetings to mine group gold don't just happen. Because group sessions produce results that cannot be gained in any other way, careful planning of the meeting structure is a must. An effective structure aids the facilitation process, ensures optimum participation from group members, and greatly increases the chances of cashing in on the collaborative brain power of the group.

The value of structure and its positive impact on group session efficiency and effectiveness is demonstrated by recounting a popular TV commercial for oil filters.

The setting for the commercial is an auto repair garage. A mechanic is in the foreground. An automobile with its hood up and chains from an overhead pulley running into the engine compartment can be seen in the background. The mechanic yells over his shoulder, "OK, take it away, Joe." The chains tighten, and the car's engine is lifted out and swung over to a workbench.

The camera focuses on the mechanic in the foreground as he says, "You know, this guy didn't have to spend $800 on this expensive engine repair job. If he had spent $6 twice a year for one of these (he holds up an oil filter as the camera zooms in), all of this could have been avoided." As the camera pulls back and refocuses on the mechanic, he emphatically states, "The choice is yours. You can pay me now, or you can pay me later!"

So it is with planning the structure of a group session. If you are too busy to make a small investment in planning time (a $6 oil filter), you may have to suffer the consequences of wasting everyone's time and energy in an unproductive session (the $800 cost for a blown engine). Sooner or later, you will pay dearly for not planning the session's structure.

The "you can pay me now, or you can pay me later" illustration drives home the message that a little time and effort invested in up-front planning will be paid back—with interest—in time and effort saved both during and after the session.

Bluntly put, taking time to plan the structure of a group session is not a discretionary activity for the meeting caller; it is a non-negotiable obligation.

PLANNING THE STRUCTURE OF A GROUP SESSION

Before a manager can think about the process aspects of the session, he or she must focus on five questions:

1. What are the session's purpose and desired outcomes?

2. Is a group session necessary?

3. Who should attend the session?

4. What is the macrocomposition of the group and what can be learned about its potential "chemistry?"

5. What is the agenda content and the topical flow?

These five questions form a planning checklist and need to be answered in the sequence presented here. By following this format each time, the basic structure of a group session will be successfully formulated. Let's look at each question in detail.

What Are the Session's Purpose and Desired Outcomes?

A clear understanding of what is to be accomplished is the foundation on which the entire session rests. If the group leader cannot clarify the session's purpose and desired outcomes before bringing the participants together, that person does not deserve the right to hold a group session! That's how fundamental the purpose and desired outcomes are. My current passion for establishing the purpose and desired outcomes of a session was first kindled by the Zenger–Miller organization's excellent *Group Action Workshop.*[1]

Without a clear purpose statement and succinctly defined desired outcomes developed beforehand, the manager takes a giant step toward meeting failure. Basically the stage has been set for meeting anarchy.

Lacking a purpose and explicit desired outcomes, the session will meander. Confusion, irritation, acrimony, and endless arguments over "why are we here?" and "what are we trying to accomplish?" will abound. Group members' time will be wasted (the high cost of wasted time was well-documented in Chapter 2).

The undercurrent of discontent and exasperation will become a tidal wave; many participants will either tune out completely or fail to contribute their best efforts. The mood of the meeting will not be conducive to success.

If there is no stated purpose and set of desired outcomes to help a meeting refocus and get back on track when necessary, where the session ends up is where it ends up. Whether or not the correct issues were addressed, or, if they were, were they addressed properly, is anybody's guess. That profound twentieth-century philosopher, Yogi Berra, said it best: "If you don't know where you are going, you'll wind up someplace else and not know how you got there."

Purpose.   The purpose of the session is the reason for bringing the attendees together whether face-to-face, via video conference or via teleconference. Zeroing in on the session's purpose is not difficult to do. By completing the following phrase, "To share and process information relative to   . .," an incisive purpose can be written every time.

For example, a manager conferring with his or her staff on the subject of holding a team-building session could state the purpose for coming together as: "To share and process information relative to holding a family group team-building session." Or, a team leader could state the purpose for calling together her quality improvement team members as: "To share and process information relative to evaluating our Continuous Quality Improvement [CQI] projects."

Desired Outcomes.   The desired outcomes (or, as they are sometimes referred to in the literature, the goals, objectives, or outputs) are specific statements identifying what is to be accomplished during the time spent in the session. The desired outcomes do four things:

1. They create common expectations among all participants,

2. They provide focus for the session,

3. They define the type of session being conducted, and

4. They provide a benchmark against which the actual outcomes can be compared to gain a sense of the session's productivity.

In his comedy routine, Woody Allen asks, "How can you possibly be lost if you don't have a final destination?" Similarly, in workshops I pose the question: "How can you tell if your group session has gotten off course if you haven't defined your desired outcomes?" The answer to both questions is the same, "You can't!"

However, when the desired outcomes are agreed upon, all group members have a target: a reference point for monitoring and controlling the direction of the session.

The misuse of targets is graphically illustrated by this tale. A traveler was passing through Coshocton, a small town in central Ohio. As he entered town, he saw a big billboard. On the white portion, someone had drawn a target and right through the middle of the target was an arrow—a bull's eye. He went down the road a bit and there was a big, broad oak tree with a white target on it, and right through the middle was another bull's eye. All over Coshocton, there were bull's eyes.

The traveler thought to himself, "Somewhere in this town there's one heckuva marksman and I'm going to find him." By asking a lot of people he finally did. The marksman turned out to be the son of a local farmer.

The traveler said, "Young man, you certainly have a great gift. No matter what the town folk say about farm boys, you have developed a unique skill. Tell me, how did you get to be such a champion marksman?"

The boy answered, "There's nothing to it. First you shoot, then you draw the target!"

Thousands of meetings are held each day following the farm boy's philosophy. Meet first, then decide after the fact that whatever was achieved was on target, then declare the session a rousing success. This process might be described as "how to always feel great about what was accomplished regardless of what it was."

Meetings are serious business. Don't waste people's time and the organization's money. As a miner of group gold, set your desired outcomes (targets) first and then facilitate team effort toward the achievement of those outcomes.

As Jay aptly points out, "The most important question you should ask is: 'What is the meeting intended to achieve?' ... 'When it is over, how shall I judge whether it was a success or failure?'—but unless you have a very clear requirement from the meeting, there is a grave danger that it will be a waste of everyone's time."[2]

For clarity, keep the desired outcomes as brief as possible. Try writing the desired outcomes as simple sentences using a subject/verb format. Desired outcomes are written in the past tense so that going into the session the team already has a feeling of accomplishment. Examples of session outcomes are:

➢ Program schedule revised.

➢ Testing results communicated.

➢ Next year's budget finalized.

➢ Pricing change approved.

➢ Curriculum analysis completed.

➢ Transportation policy established.

In conjunction with the purpose statement developed earlier, the desired outcome for the team-building meeting could be: "Team-building GO/NO GO decision made." The desired outcome for the meeting to evaluate CQI projects could be: "Three improvement projects selected."

It also helps to write the desired outcomes on flip chart paper and post them for all meeting attendees to refer to during the session.

Is a Group Session Necessary?

Once the purpose and outcomes of a group session have been crystallized by the supervisor, the most fundamental of all questions must be asked: "Is a group session really required?"

This question must always be answered second, not first. A manager cannot know if a meeting is necessary until the purpose and desired outcomes have been itemized. Reversing these first two steps creates the deadly trap of a self-fulfilling prophecy. In other words, "I've decided to have a meeting. Now that I've determined I need a meeting, I'll figure out my reason for calling it and what outcomes I hope to achieve."

Eliminate this trap by sticking to the planning sequence advocated here. First, specify the purpose and desired outcomes of a session. Then, determine if there are other ways of achieving the desired outcomes without bringing people together inside the four walls of a conference room. If the desired outcomes can be accomplished by some means other than conducting a meeting, don't hold a meeting!

A common type of fruitless meeting is when a manager calls a session to be briefed by several people who report directly to the manager but whose work depends little (or not at all) on what each of the others do. While a manager may feel this is an effective use of his or her time, the people called to such a meeting usually will resent what seems to them to be a waste of their time.

As part of the hundreds of workshops I've conducted at Xerox on the principles of mining group gold, I've routinely asked the participants, "What percentage of the meetings that you convene, or attend at the request of another person, do you believe are unnecessary?" The responses consistently have fallen in the 15 to 25 percent range, indicating that many meetings are unnecessary.

In a September workshop that I conducted, a manager stated that the day before he had received from his boss the entire schedule of staff meetings for the upcoming year. The manager's comments were interesting.

"Fifty-two staff meetings every Tuesday from 7:45 A.M. to 9:45 A.M. whether we need them or not. We've been told to post the list on our walls immediately. So now we've generated a self-fulfilling prophecy. Three-and-one-half months before the new year, it has been declared that we will hold 52 staff meetings next year; and I guarantee we will. There have been at least a half dozen times so far this year when we should have canceled or measurably reduced the time devoted to our staff meetings. We didn't; we've stuck to our schedule week after week like it was a decree from heaven."

The moral of this story is: Even if a series of recurring meetings is set up in advance, do not get locked in to holding every single one just because its day has arrived. The world will not come to an end if a staff meeting scheduled three months ago is canceled or significantly shortened due to a lack of pertinent subjects or because of other business that is more important.

Always remain flexible and adhere to the principle that states: "Regularly scheduled meetings should be held irregularly whenever appropriate."

Regarding the productivity-robbing power of unnecessary meetings, O'Neill provides a most interesting example.

> In this particular factory, . . . output averaged 10 percent more for every weekend compared with weekdays. Further, the night shift figures were at least 2 percent higher than the day levels.
>
> [After analysis of a number of potential causes,] management interference was proven to be the culprit. Managers did "drop-in" at all hours, but they were normally present only during the morning and afternoon. When on site, though, they held many meetings. . . . Most meetings involved the attendance of line supervisors (and not infrequently, off-shift operatives). Were the operatives, left unsupervised, simply slacking during the meetings? This suggestion was ruled out on two counts. First it was just not compatible with the general climate in the plant, nor with the output bonus scheme that operated.
>
> An analysis of delays showed that many standard delays took longer to resolve on day-shift than on weekends. The answer was now clear: during the day-shift, the line supervisors and shift managers, frequently called away into meetings, were not around to deal with an emergency, or when quick production decisions were required. Their attendance at meetings was building delay into decision making.
>
> Most meetings were held in the morning, but there were still several in the afternoon—which often went into the evening. On weekends there were no meetings at all, and this explained a production pattern that went something like this: day-shift lowest output; afternoon-shift at least 2 percent higher; night-shift 4 to 5 percent higher than days; weekends 10 percent higher than

normal days; long "shut-down" weekends, 12–14 percent higher than days.[3]

Alternatives to Group Sessions. The figures in Chapter 2 vividly portrayed the high cost of holding even seemingly routine meetings. A great many important matters can be quite satisfactorily resolved by using alternatives other than the common practice of sharing and processing information in groups. Therefore, it is wise to consider all of the following possibilities before rushing off to organize one more potentially unnecessary meeting. Avoid meetings by using:

➤ Telephone calls.

➤ Round-robin memos.

➤ Electronic communications including e-mail, groupware communications, and faxes.

➤ Informal conversations/hall talk.

➤ "FYI" copies of meeting minutes to a select number of people who have a need to know but don't need to attend the meeting.

➤ One-on-one conversations.

➤ Voice mail (VMAX).

➤ Executive summaries.

➤ Bulletin board messages in high-traffic areas.

➤ Newspapers/newsletters for one-way general information sharing.

Jim Stoffel, vice president and general manager for one of the Xerox Business Units, emphasizes his dislike of unnecessary meetings by often repeating the following comment to his management team. "When it is not necessary to hold a meeting, it is necessary not to hold the meeting!"

Situations That Usually Require Group Sessions. Given the underlying circumstances of the situation, having a meeting may be the only way to proceed. A group session offers an interplay of ideas, a variety of viewpoints, and a commitment to action that evolves through group participation rather than from outside imposition. The important common denominator for meetings, as demonstrated by the following list, is that the situation requires group action or participation. With this thought in mind, situations that require a meeting include the following:

> No one person has sufficient information to make a quality decision.

> Acceptance of an idea, program, or decision by the group is critical to its implementation.

> The topic is complex, and it is critical that everyone has the same understanding of the information and data.

> Conflicting views need to be reconciled.

> People receiving and having to act on the information are interdependent.

> The issue being faced is unstructured; for example, what information is required, where to find it, how to find it, etc., are unknown.

> Information needs to be communicated and immediately processed among a number of people.

> A synergistic effect is likely to be produced from bringing a group together to process the issue.

> Group information processing tools such as affinity diagrams, fishbone diagrams, decision trees, etc., are to be used.

In any event, if you are convinced that a group session is necessary, you are obliged to plan and facilitate the session in a manner that neither wastes your time and energy nor that of the participants.

Who Should Attend?

Once the purpose and outcomes are defined and it's clear that group action or participation is required, effective planning requires that you carefully consider the question: "Who are the appropriate people to invite to this particular meeting?"

The general principle for choosing group session partici-pants is: Select the fewest number of people required to achieve the desired outcomes! When there are too many cooks in the kitchen, you either don't get the meal out or it takes you twice as long. There may be a good reason for including one or two individuals who may not directly contribute to the achieve-ment of the desired outcomes, but the decision to include them should be a conscious and rational one. The fatal mistake made by many managers and chairpersons at this stage of the plan-ning process is to use the shotgun approach and invite a "cast of thousands" to ensure that all the right people will be present. This random and indiscriminate approach to selecting meeting attendees does not guarantee the presence of the appropriate people and sows the seeds of a facilitation nightmare.

There is a maxim about meetings that says: "If you want a job done poorly, turn it over to a large group because perfor-mance is inversely proportionate to group size." Hymowitz, quoting several businessmen in an article for *The Wall Street Journal*, provides a graphic example of this maxim.

> The more who attend a meeting, the slimmer the chances any work will get done. "Everyone wants some air time— if only to show how persuasive they can be—and meet-ings with 10 or more participants tend to digress from their formal agendas and run hours longer than they should," says Robert Kelly, a professor at Carnegie–Mellon University's business school.
>
> Harry Thompson, president of Gen Corp's reinforced-plastics division, took along just two associates for a technical meeting with a customer—only to face a room filled with twenty-five managers. "The issues we needed to resolve weren't that deep, but they had people from every level of the organization, and each of them had to put their two-cents in," he says. The result: the meeting Mr. Thompson figured would last two hours took all day.[4]

Unnecessary attendees, those who have no real interest or stake in the session's desired outcomes, pose a twofold facili-tation dilemma. First, this expansion in group size exacerbates the facilitation task. Meeting dynamics are simpler and easier to manage with a group of five than they are with a group of 10 or 12. Second, people invited to a meeting who are not keenly interested in the desired outcomes tend to be disruptive. In the great majority of cases, these people are not trying to be disruptive and don't realize they are detrimental to the session's progress; however, facilitation complications develop because of their attendance.

It's only natural for nonessential meeting members to feel compelled to contribute. But because the subject matter is, at best, only of marginal interest to them, these "extra invitees" try to shape the meeting—either consciously or unconsciously—to their own needs. They interject thoughts, ideas, facts, and opinions that are irrelevant to the main discussion. They are not working to help accomplish the session's desired outcomes because they are not committed to them.

Often, because they are frustrated with how little they are deriving from the meeting, unnecessary attendees either visibly withdraw (push away from the table, read mail, write responses to memos they have received, fidget, or keep leaving and coming back) or they develop into irritable, cantankerous participants.

Most of these facilitation difficulties are brought about because of lack of attention to a key planning question, "who should attend?" If you are preparing to hold a group session, don't stack the deck against yourself by inviting unnecessary people.

The selection process may be as straightforward as having the entire family group attend the session, or as complicated as including family group members along with attendees from other departments and even from outside the company. Selection of attendees must never be random or left to chance. The need to make certain that the right people are at the meeting is amusingly reinforced by Soden.

In order to assure maximum results from a reasonable and necessary meeting, a concentrated effort must be placed upon inviting participants with the authority to make decisions. Having unnecessary corporate bodies (corp-ses) at a meeting often means unwarranted discussions and delays. Meetings of the board can become unproductive meetings of the bored. Corporations can end up in a situation similar to that of a British university: A wealthy benefactor's will provided a trust fund of continuing financial support to the university on the condition that the deceased continue as a member of the board of trustees and that the embalmed body be present at meetings. This quiescent attendee was recorded as 'present but not voting.' Nonessential attendees at corporate meetings are useless.[5]

The selection of attendees must never be random or left to chance. The considerations presented next are useful in helping to ensure that, while a number of people may be contemplated, only those deemed essential to the attainment and implementation of the desired outcomes are invited.

Selecting Appropriate Attendees. Think small; as Soden pointed out, nonessential people are useless. Unless there is a solid reason for inviting a person to a session, an invitation should not be extended. The following checklist focuses on justifying each attendee's need to be at the session and, as such, helps screen out unnecessary people. Remember, no one will feel neglected or overlooked if excluded from a meeting with a desired outcome in which that person has no particular concern. In fact, you may receive thanks for giving the person a gift of time. An individual should be considered a necessary meeting participant if he or she:

➤ Possesses critical information, knowledge, or expertise pertinent to the subject area under consideration.

➤ Has a stake in the final outcome. That is, this individual will be directly impacted by what is decided, and his or her commitment is required for successful implementation.

➤ Has responsibility for implementing whatever is decided.

➤ Has the authority and responsibility to make the final decision about what to do.

➤ Needs to better understand the situation in order to reduce his or her fear of the unknown.

➤ Is one of the members of the total family group, task force, committee, or council. (This is a requirement whenever the entire group must get together.)

➤ Possesses contrary viewpoints that will stimulate discussion, produce critical thinking, and eliminate the dysfunctional behavior of groupthink.

➤ Needs the developmental experience. That is, this person needs to acquire the knowledge, skills, or processes being shared and/or needs to meet and network with the other participants.

➤ Needs to be present because of his or her position in the hierarchy or because of the politics of the situation. (This person may not be relevant to achieving the desired outcomes of the particular meeting; however, the individual may be very relevant to the success or failure of the overall project. Respect the politics of the situation when necessary.)

➤ Has the authority and/or influence to act as a credible representative for a number of people, thus holding down the size of the meeting without compromising its productivity.

Remember the simple ground rule: No justification for attendance, no attendance. However, if you have justified someone to attend a session who is not a regular member, you need to brief the person ahead of time on: why he or she was invited; your expectations for their participation; and, any groundrules the group employs. This prepares the invitee for maximum contribution.

Eliminating People from Ongoing Sessions. The checklist given above is not limited just to screening and selecting members for newly planned group sessions. It is also an excellent tool for reviewing the membership of all current, ongoing meetings. If you are responsible for conducting such ongoing sessions, use the checklist to justify attendance. As many as 30 percent of current attendees may be eliminated because they are not justified; occasionally the checklist also could lead to adding another person or two because it points up a previously unrecognized opportunity to strengthen the meeting.

Two questions that I am asked over and over again are, "How do I get rid of someone who has been a regular attendee at my meeting but who is not really needed?" and "What do I do about the person who insists on coming against my better judgment?"

First, eliminating someone from an ongoing session does not mean eliminating that person from the information loop. This fact must be made clear, as illustrated by the following examples:

> "Bob, I'll make sure you stay on the distribution list for the minutes of the meeting. If you have any questions or issues about what you read, call me directly."

> "Grace, I know Dwight has the same interests as you do. I'll make sure he calls you after each meeting and tells you what took place. Then you can share your views with him."

> "Chuck, feel free to call anyone on the committee if there is something you want brought up in future meetings."

> "Reynaldo, I'll send you an advance copy of the agenda each month. If there is something of great interest to you, we can work out arrangements for you to attend."

Second, be forthright and friendly when discussing the issue with the other person. Since people generally preserve the fiction that they are overworked and dislike serving on committees and project teams in the first place, usually it is not hard to secure their consent to stay away. Point out that you are, in fact, giving them a gift of time.

Third, always remain open-minded. If people present sound reasons why their attendance is critical, thank them for their insight and indicate that you're looking forward to their full participation in future sessions.

Finally, if someone who truly is nonessential blows his or her stack and insists on being involved, back off. If a person has not been an abnormally disruptive force in previous sessions, let him or her continue attending the meetings.

An important finding from research on meeting effectiveness conducted by Oppenheim furnishes a fitting conclusion to this topic.

> Meetings without the right people are likely to be unproductive. Meetings with too many people—or people from too many different levels—can also limit productivity. In fact, senior managers across all five of the organizations surveyed agreed that, in their organizations, the primary cause of unproductive meetings was the inappropriate selection of participants. Middle managers were less attuned to the importance of this, but they also thought it significant.[6]

What Is the Macrocomposition of the Group and Its Potential Chemistry?

Once the attendance list is firmed up, step back and look at the group from a "macro" perspective. You probably will know many, if not all, of the participants (either personally or by reputation). By taking this "macro" point of view, you can gain insight into the potential chemistry of the group.

In teaching, counseling, and coaching managers on the principles advocated in this book, I have been surprised by a consistent finding. With few exceptions, group chemistry is totally ignored by managers, chairpersons, and group facilitators as they plan group sessions. But when this key step is brought to their attention, they invariably see the merit of it and can give personal testimony to situations where ignoring chemistry led to problems that ruined the productivity of a session.

Advanced thinking about the group's chemistry is critical. It is a "distant early warning" process that provides pre-meeting insight into the potential dynamics among meeting invitees and the positive or negative effect that these potential dynamics could have on achieving the session's desired outcomes. For example, a particular group may be very dedicated, hardworking, and enthusiastic about the session and its desired outcomes; this group could be very productive on a task assigned to run from 4:30 to 6:15 P.M. On the flip side, a 4:30 to 6:15 P.M. task planned for a cynical, unenthusiastic, and disinterested group may be an unproductive exercise.

Assessing potential chemistry does not imply that you must serve as the group psychologist and try to "psych out" the group's behavior. Rather, you should make an effort to anticipate how people might react to the meeting content and to each other once the session begins. In this way, you will be prepared to deal with any problems that could arise.

One manager, when asked about the chemistry of a task force she was chairing, gave this humorous response: "Oh, there is a tremendous feeling of togetherness on the task force. Everyone is equally unhappy."

Anticipating group chemistry as a valuable main planning step is reinforced further by the following example. Let's say that a group session includes two attendees with radically different viewpoints on how to tackle a vexing departmental problem. Unfortunately, neither one is particularly open-minded about the other's point of view. Anticipating this situation will not eliminate it, but it does alert you to potentially disruptive behavior and allow you to be prepared to facilitate a sticky situation. This means allowing each member an equal say and making sure differences are defined in terms of issues, not personalities.

Much tension can be diffused if you say something like, "Let me see if I understand the issue here. You, Hal, think that the best way to approach this is to. . .; whereas you, Bette, would like to see us. . . . Am I right? Good. Now, as a group, let's list the pros and cons of both proposals."

The following guidelines will help you gauge group chemistry before the meeting begins.

➤ Has the group worked together before? If so, what strengths existed in their interaction patterns that should be encouraged now? What should be changed as much as possible?

➤ Who probably will be enthusiastic about attending? Who most likely will be turned off?

➤ Which people have had interaction difficulties in the past?

65

> ➤ Who—potentially—could be disruptive and in what way?

> ➤ What is the overall demeanor of the group probably going to be? Aggressive, laid-back, fun-loving, serious, emotional, analytical?

> ➤ What will be the general degree of support, or resistance, to each topic or issue?

> ➤ Which people carry the greatest influence based on position, expertise, tenure, charisma, etc.? Would any of these people have the tendency to dominate the discussion or take over control of the session?

> ➤ Could differences in status among attendees inhibit those lower in the hierarchy from being active participants without facilitation encouragement?

For some questions, only a "best guess" estimate may be possible prior to the session. That's fine. Remember, you are not trying to psychoanalyze the people; you are simply looking ahead, anticipating potential trouble spots in the group's chemistry, and preparing yourself to facilitate a problem if it should arise.

You might anticipate that, due to his position and charisma, Arnold will dominate the discussion and push his solutions on the group. So, drawing from the section in Chapter 8 entitled "Dealing with Disruptive Behavior," you plan your methods for dealing with Arnold if he starts to dominate. You're ready and confident. But, guess what? For whatever reason, Arnold turns out to be a model participant. Great! It is far better to be prepared for a problem that never arises than to be unprepared for one that must be handled "on the fly" without any forethought.

What Is the Agenda Content and Topical Flow?

Research has shown that group sessions with a clear-cut agenda tend to be better focused, significantly more effective, and achieve more specific results than meetings without an agenda.

How many agendas have you prepared or seen like the one shown in Exhibit 4–1? More than likely, far too many. The example in Exhibit 4–1 is not really an agenda at all. It is nothing more than a crib sheet of time allocations, topics, and topic leaders. This type of "agenda" is invariably prepared by the manager for the sole convenience of the manager. What real impact will it have on group session effectiveness and productivity? The answer is: None!

What are the key particulars of the session? What's the purpose? What are the desired outcomes? What meeting roles do the attendees have? Is Susan Hart just going to share information on the Hiring Plan or is this an information processing topic with a decision required at the end? Are the topics in priority order? Etc. Etc. This, all to common, "agenda" doesn't communicate anything and doesn't provide any mechanism for in-session meeting management.

Dr. Alton Bartlett, chairman of the department of management at the University of South Florida in Tampa, has spoken about agenda power to executives for many years. His message is important.

> Chefs use recipes, contractors use blueprints, orchestra conductors use sheet music, and pilots use flight plans. Each of these highly skilled professionals relies on structured documents to help them achieve their desired outcomes. But many meeting leaders try to do their job without agendas. Why should they be any different? It is not a simple crib sheet of a list of topics to cover. An

Exhibit 4–1: TYPICAL AGENDA

Agenda for February 14, 199X		
8:00 A.M. – 12:30 P.M.		
15 min.	Introduction	Andy Johnson
75 min.	Cash Flow Analysis Q-II	Joyce Lao
45 min.	Travel Budget	Fred Nichols
15 min.	Break	All
90 min.	Hiring Plans	Susan Hart
30 min.	Round the Table	All

agenda is the construction plan for the session. It is the most valuable tool to keep the "group mind" focused, on track, and on time as it pursues achievement of the session's desired outcomes. To quote a well-known commercial: "Don't leave home without it."[7]

There is no standard format for an agenda; however, there are fundamental principles that, when practiced, can significantly enhance its development and use.

Agenda-Building for Multi-topic Meetings. The staff meeting is the most common type of meeting. Staff meetings cover a wide range of agenda subjects that usually are unrelated (or only partially related) to each other. For example, a staff meeting might cover "Planning the department's vacation schedule," which is unrelated to the next topic, "Choosing a name for the departmental newsletter." Other sessions that are similar to staff meetings include steering committee meetings; board meetings like school boards, boards of directors, or boards of trustees; regularly scheduled operations reviews; various kinds of council meetings; and the like.

Before reading on, look at Exhibit 4–2. This shows the recommended agenda format for planning the structure of "staff-type" group sessions. Also, review Exhibit 4–3 to get an idea of what the completed agenda will look like. After you have reviewed the sample agendas, look at the principles for structuring the multi-topic meeting.

1. *Prominently display the key particulars.* The standard header for any agenda should be the key particulars, including the title or name of the meeting, the date of the meeting, its start and end time, and its location.

2. *Note participants who are given key roles.* There are four key roles that must be routinely assigned at every meeting. The fifth role, that of scribe (or recorder), can be assigned when needed. The key roles are described in the last section of this chapter.

3. *Classify agenda topics.* Agenda topics should be classified as either information sharing or information processing. Information-sharing items are pure information giving. They are

Exhibit 4–2: AGENDA

KEY PARTICULARS
Name of Meeting:
Date:
Start Time: End time:
Building: Room:

KEY ROLES
Primary Facilitator:
Secondary Facilitators:
Timekeeper:
Minute Taker:

Information Sharing	Plan		Actual	Information Processing	Desired Outcomes
	Time	Clock	Clock		

Exhibit 4–3: AGENDA

KEY PARTICULARS

Name of Meeting:	Administrative Staff Meeting		
Date:	November 14, 199X		
Start Time:	2:00 P.M.	End time:	5:00 P.M.
Building:	Admin.	Room:	703

KEY ROLES

Primary Facilitator:	Wyatt Webb
Secondary Facilitators:	All
Timekeeper:	Tony Laterza
Minute Taker:	Clymon Lee

Information Sharing	Plan		Actual Clock	Information Processing	Desired Outcomes
	Time	Clock			
Informal Warm-Up	5 min.	2:00–2:05			
Agenda Review (W. Webb)	5 min.	2:05–2:10			
"Do Better" Reminders (W. Webb)	2 min.	2:10–2:12			
Curriculum Committee Progress (W. Webb)	3 min.	2:12–2:15			
Fund Raising Results (D. Morano)	5 min.	2:15–2:20			
Open House Update (S. Van Duser)	5 min.	2:20–2:25			
	15 min.	2:25–2:40		1. Pool Safety: Rules and Regulations (T. O'Hara)	Recommended Pool Safety Plan Approval
	15 min.	2:40–2:55		2. District Asbestos Removal (P. Chirico)	Time Line for Removal Finalized
	20 min.	2:55–3:15		3. Teacher Negotiations Update • Teacher Positions (A. Rosen) • Board Responses (A. Rosen)	Current Issues Statused and Discussed
Break	10 min.	3:15–3:25			
	50 min.	3:25–4:15		4. Principal Hiring Process: Criteria Development (M. Keller Cogan)	Set of Hiring Criteria Developed and Agreed To
	30 min.	4:15–4:45		5. AIDS Instruction K–12: Infusion into the Curriculum (M. Garcia)	Task Force Guidelines and Expectations Formulated
	15 min.	4:45–5:00		6. Wrap-up (W. Webb)	Decisions Reviewed Action Items Reviewed Leftover Items Dispensed Session Critiqued

FYI only; that is, they are short, simple, relatively noncontroversial bits of information that can be covered in less than five minutes. They are meant to inform others by providing one-way communication.

During the information-sharing section of the meeting, group members can seek clarification to ensure that they understand what is being shared. However, discussion and processing are not permitted.

Information-processing subjects require in-depth discussion, debate, analysis, problem solving, decision making, and/or action planning. These are often complex, controversial subjects that require group members to "roll up their sleeves and dig in." Some items may be covered in five or ten minutes; others may take many hours or even days.

4. *Batch information-sharing items; handle them early.* Most information-sharing items should be pulled together and treated as a block of information to be shared at the beginning of the session. This gets everyone involved and energizes the session. Also, the sharing portion quite often provides important data that can be used during the processing of the subjects that come later. If the meeting planner feels that an information-sharing item is more strategically placed by putting it in the middle or near the end of the session, that's fine.

5. *Decide on a time block for covering all information-sharing items.* Make a quick assessment of the content of the information-sharing items and assign a *maximum* block of time to cover the entire group. The time allocated will vary depending on the number of people present, the number of items, and the level of detail at which people share their information.

6. *Make certain that each information-processing topic has its own desired outcome.* Effective planning of a meeting's structure requires that each discrete information processing item has a clearly stated desired outcome linked to it. The desired outcome is critical, since it defines what should be accomplished after the information processing is completed.

7. *Sequence information-processing topics to enhance information flow.* Arrange processing topics sequentially so that as decisions are made on early items those will, in turn, provide relevant input to assist in resolving succeeding issues. If there is a choice, do not start information processing with the most

difficult or controversial subject; and, whenever possible, end with a topic that will tend to unify the group.

8. *Determine times for each information-processing topic.* A tricky part of planning the agenda is to plan the time frame for each processing item. The guiding consideration should be the desired outcome. Be realistic and honest when setting time frames. Ask, "What is the best estimate of the time we will need to achieve the stated desired outcome?" When estimating time frames, take into account the likelihood of conflict, the amount of up-front briefing that will be required, the degree of familiarity the members have with each other, the number of people involved, and any other similar considerations.

9. *Involve all participants.* Distribute a copy of the agenda at least three working days in advance of the meeting. When creating the agenda, take advantage of every opportunity to obtain input from the meeting participants. This generates a sense of shared ownership and commitment to the session. From the meeting members' perspective, this action moves the meeting from being Tom's session or Rebecca's session to being OUR session. Exhibit 4-4 can be used as a resource for gathering agenda items from group members.

Exhibit 4-4: MEETING PLANNING WORKSHEET
For Submitting Topics to the Meeting Planner

Name of Meeting: _____

Date: _____ Time: _____

Name of Person Initiating a Topic	Topic	IS	IP	Desired Outcome	Time Required

IS = Information Sharing   IP = Information Processing

10. *Write a cover memo to be sent out with each agenda.* While the agenda is the basic work plan of the meeting, it may not fully communicate everything about the session. A concise cover memo (one page maximum) can clarify, supplement, and/or highlight the information contained in the agenda. At a minimum, set forth the following information in your cover memo.

Provide the first and last names of all invitees. This usually is shown as the distribution list for the memo and agenda.

Highlight the purpose of the session. Staff meetings, as well as other multi-topic meetings, all have the same purpose: *To share and process information of mutual interest and concern to all members in attendance.*

Note the names of all who are expected to take a lead role in the discussion and analysis of a topic and indicate what data and information they are expected to have available at the session.

Provide a crisp synopsis of the current status for any complex, ongoing subjects and give clear and concise instructions for any pre-work that is sent out with the agenda.

Agenda-Building for Single- or Dual-Topic Meetings. Problem-solving and decision-making meetings tend to focus on one or two highly interrelated, topics. An example of a single-topic agenda is shown in Exhibit 4–5.

In order to solve a vexing problem or make a difficult decision, a number of sessions may need to be convened around the same issue. However, each meeting in the series needs to have a short purpose statement, a clear statement of the desired outcomes, the assignment of the four standard roles to group members, and an agenda of key steps (with clock times) for working through that specific meeting.

Since information sharing (IS) and information processing (IP) both focus on the same subject, they can be shown together but with IS and IP notations to distinguish the agenda steps. Notice that the desired outcomes pertain to the entire meeting; in other words, the entire session is focused on achieving a limited number of very specific outcomes.

A cover memo to accompany the single-item agenda is just as critical as it is for the multi-topic agenda. Developing a meaningful agenda sets the stage for productive facilitation.

Exhibit 4–5: AGENDA, SALES COST REDUCTION TASK FORCE

KEY PARTICULARS		KEY ROLES	
Date:	April 24, 199X	Primary Facilitator:	Carol Koneff
Start:	9:30 A.M.	Secondary Facilitators:	All
End:	11:30 A.M.	Timekeeper:	Don D'Amico
Building:	162	Minute Taker:	Fred Kemp
Room:	Exec.-"C"		

Purpose of Session:

• To share and process information relative to reducing sales costs.

Desired Outcomes:

• Potential solutions for reducing sales costs identified.
• Three potential solutions for detailed action planning selected.

9:30–9:35	IS	Informal socializing and warm-up
9:35–9:40	IS	Review purpose, desired outcomes, and agenda
9:40–9:50	IS	Review work completed last week
		A. Agreed-to problem statement
		B. Finalized list of causes driving up sales costs
9:50–10:00	IS	Brainstorm potential solutions to reduce or eliminate causes of rising sales costs
10:00–10:15	IP	Clarify items, combine similar solutions
10:15–11:10	IP	Discuss pros and cons of solutions and reach consensus on top six to eight
11:10–11:20	IP	Use criteria matrix to evaluate the six to eight solutions and choose top three
11:20–11:30	IP	Wrap-up, next steps, and critique
		A. Decisions reviewed
		B. Action items reviewed
		C. Next steps covered
		D. Session critiqued

IS = Information Sharing   IP = Information Processing

Agenda-Building Tips for Planning Breaks. In today's fast-paced world, managers and other attendees feel a strong need to keep in contact with their job outside the confines of the meeting room. After more than a few hours, people get restless. They begin to feel disconnected from their job and get concerned—often unnecessarily—that the normal flow of work will be disrupted by their absence. As a consequence, individuals are seen running in and out to check their voice mail, to hold a brief conference call, or to follow-up on an item that came up during the session. With participants coming and going, the session loses focus and energy, plus the desired outcomes are placed at risk.

I've learned, through the school of hard knocks, that you can't fight this phenomenon. You have to go with the flow and plan for it. I've learned that for any session scheduled to run for a half day or more, it is imperative to plan a break long enough for people to attend to incidental business outside the conference room. On the surface this may seem like a sacrifice of precious in-session meeting time, but believe me, it isn't. In the long run you will have a more productive session because people will remain in the room and will be more focused and energized.

So, instead of planning a 10 or 15 minute break for mid-morning, plan one for 30 minutes. If the session is to last all day, do the same for mid-afternoon. At the beginning of the session, explain your expectations for the break(s). Then, hold the break as close to the scheduled time as possible and don't shorten it. However, when the break time is over, restart the session promptly to send the strong signal that both the meeting content and schedule are important.

UNDERSTANDING THE KEY ROLES IN EVERY MEETING

Every meeting must have four key role assignments: primary facilitator, secondary facilitators, timekeeper, and minute taker. A fifth role, that of the scribe (or recorder), may not be assigned at every meeting but, when needed, the scribe is central to the success of the meeting.

Primary Facilitator

This is the primary person who focuses on the *process dynamics of the group session*. He or she stays keenly aware of how things are done in the session and intervenes to preserve the integrity and disciplined use of the processes described in this book. Initially, the manager, committee chairperson, or cross-functional team leader responsible for calling and planning the session assumes this role.

This book is written from the perspective of the *formal manager or head person as primary facilitator*. Therefore, since the manager, chairperson, or team leader in most cases also will contribute significantly to the content of the discussion, he or she must verbally indicate what is happening any time there is a switch in roles from *primary facilitator* (focused on process) to *manager* (focused on content) or back again. This switching of hats is for the benefit of other participants so they are not confused about the role the manager is operating in at any time.

As other group members acquire facilitation skills, the role of primary facilitator can be rotated among them. These people then will have to "switch hats" between being primary facilitators and contributing team members.

Secondary Facilitators

An effective and productive group session cannot be achieved by one primary facilitator—even if it is the manager—trying to direct a herd of wild horses intent on ignoring the purpose, desired outcomes, and agenda; resisting any process discipline; making no effort to listen and understand each other; and trampling on each other to see who can control the session.

Once the primary facilitator is designated, everyone else in attendance is assigned the role of secondary facilitator. The secondary facilitators share the responsibility for a productive meeting with the primary facilitator by doing two things: (1) monitoring themselves so that they minimize their own disruptive behaviors, and (2) intervening quickly to facilitate any productivity-robbing activities as soon as they occur.

Typical examples of secondary facilitation, where a person other than the primary facilitator can intervene to help the group process, include the following:

➤ Alerting the group whenever it is straying from its desired outcomes. This can be facilitated by setting up a code word that everyone in the group can use to tell the group it is off course. One group I worked with used the word "weeds" to indicate that it had strayed off the main path it had agreed to take. The use of the word added some fun to their otherwise tense sessions and helped the members stay focused on their desired outcomes.

➤ Stepping in to handle the disruptive behavior of another group member (side conversations, domination by one member, gate-closings, rambling, etc.).

➤ Providing input that the discussion has been reduced to nit-picking irrelevant details and that there is a need to refocus on the broader issues at hand.

➤ Pointing out that consensus seems to have been reached implicitly but the discussion is dragging on, then suggesting that the manager (in the role of facilitator) test for consensus by going around the table.

➤ Halting "the assumed right of infinite appeal." That is, stopping someone from reopening, again, without documented justification, a topic which has been thoroughly processed and decided upon by the group.

Other actions may be needed, but these highlight how easy it is to help out with the facilitation activity. The message bears repeating: Everybody is responsible for creating a productive group session.

Timekeeper

The timekeeper monitors how long the group is taking to accomplish its tasks and provides regular updates to make members aware of where they are with regard to time spent. Taking the role too seriously by being an inflexible, dogmatic timekeeper will lead to resentment toward you and the process. You are simply performing a neutral service on behalf of the group. Typically the first warning should come when half the allotted time has been used up, followed by a second warning when three-fourths of the time has been consumed, and finally a five-minute warning. At this point, if the desired outcome is not close to being achieved, the group needs to decide whether to continue processing the current topic to its conclusion or stop and move on to the next item.

Minute Taker

The minute taker sits at the table and takes notes concerning decisions reached and action item assignments (who has agreed to do what by what date). This information should be confirmed at the close of the session, typed, and distributed to all attendees (and other key individuals not at the meeting) within two working days.

Scribe

This role, also known as the recorder, is optional. Depending on the group process being used to achieve the desired outcomes, a scribe may or may not be needed at every gathering. However, when necessary, the scribe is central to the success of the meeting.

Serving as the group recorder, the scribe keeps track of what is being said in the group by writing it down on flip chart pages. When a page is completed, it is torn off the pad and taped to the wall for all to see and referred to later if necessary. During a discussion, being able to see what points have been made can help individuals analyze what has been contributed so far and build on previous ideas. The scribe should be someone skilled at organizing and synthesizing material in a visual form. Spelling and pristine neatness are not major requirements.

Recording notes on a flip chart in no way gives the scribe the right to run the meeting! The only "power of the pen" that the scribe has is to quickly write on the flip chart what people say. The scribe is NOT the primary facilitator, does NOT debate or challenge what people say for the record, and does NOT twist, edit, or in any way alter what is said versus what is recorded. If a statement is confused or complicated, the scribe asks the speaker to shorten it for the record, then records exactly what is said.

A scribe may not be needed for every session. However, when one is needed, the scribe's role should be reviewed so there are no misconceptions about what needs to be done. Since this is a tedious and tiring task, especially if there is a lot of information to record over an extended period of time, rotate the role between two people and change over every hour.

The four main structural roles should be a routine part of every meeting, and the scribe's job should be assigned as needed. Performed with spirit and dedication, these roles will dramatically enhance group session productivity. Everyone involved in these roles will feel a sense of ownership and commitment; THE meeting becomes OUR meeting!

In conclusion, Exhibit 4–6 provides a worksheet based on the important steps in planning a productive meeting. Also, a chapter summary condenses the information presented here for easy reference.

Chapter 5 presents pointers for dealing with the other half of the planning equation: planning the process of a group session.

Exhibit 4–6: GUIDESHEET FOR PLANNING THE STRUCTURE OF A GROUP SESSION

A. Purpose: What is my reason for holding this session?
I am considering holding this group session: *To share and process information relative to*

(Continued)

Exhibit 4–6: GUIDESHEET FOR PLANNING THE STRUCTURE OF A
GROUP SESSION *(Continued)*

B. **Desired Outcomes: What do I want to accomplish during this session?**
(For clarity, the session's desired outcomes should be stated as simple
sentences using the subject verb format. For example, *Hall Monitors
Nominated and Selected.*)

C. **Is a group session required to achieve my stated purpose and desired
outcomes?**   ☐ Yes   ☐ No

If no, other alternatives I could pursue would be:

D. **If a group session is required, who should attend?**
(List the names. However, your goal is to invite the smallest number of people
necessary to achieve the desired outcomes.)

E. **Stepping back and looking at the macrocomposition of the group as
determined in "D," what is the *potential chemistry* of this group?**

Potential Strengths: Areas of Positive Chemistry	Potential Problems: Areas of Negative Chemistry

Exhibit 4–6: GUIDESHEET FOR PLANNING THE STRUCTURE OF A
GROUP SESSION *(Concluded)*

What should I be prepared to do to reduce or eliminate any of the potential problems if they should arise?
(See Chapter 7, Feelings; and Chapter 8, especially the section on "Dealing with Disruptive Behaviors.")

F. **Which people do I want to assign to the following key roles?**

- Primary Facilitator:
- Secondary Facilitators: All

- Timekeeper:
- Minute Taker:
- Other:

G. **What is the agenda content and topical flow with clock times?**
(Use a separate sheet to sketch out this information. Then, depending on the type of session—multi-topic or single-topic—use the information developed in "A" through "G" and format it into an organized agenda as shown in Exhibits 4–2 or 4–5.)

CHAPTER FOUR SUMMARY

FIVE STEPS FOR PLANNING THE STRUCTURE OF A GROUP SESSION

What Are the Session's Purpose and Desired Outcomes?

Is a Group Session Necessary?

Who Should Attend?

What Is the Macrocomposition of the Group and Its Potential Chemistry?

What Is the Agenda Content and Topical Flow?

Agenda-Building for Multi-Topic Meetings
- Prominently display the key particulars
- Note participants who are given key roles
- Classify agenda topics as either information sharing or information processing
- Batch the information-sharing items; handle them early
- Decide on a time block for covering all information-sharing items
- Make certain that each information-processing topic has its own desired outcome
- Sequence information-processing topics to enhance information flow
- Determine times for each information-processing topic
- Involve all participants
- Write a cover memo to be sent out with each agenda

Agenda-Building for Single- or Dual-Topic Meetings
- Prominently display the key particulars
- Note participants who are given key roles
- Clearly state the purpose of the session
- Clearly state the desired outcomes of the session
- Arrange the agenda topics, with clock times, in the most appropriate sequence to assure the achievement of the desired outcomes

Agenda-Building Tips for Planning Breaks

UNDERSTANDING THE KEY ROLES IN EVERY MEETING

Primary Facilitator

Secondary Facilitators

Timekeeper

Minute Taker

Scribe

Notes Worksheet: DEVELOP WRITTEN RESPONSES TO THE TWO
ITEMS LISTED BELOW

What do you feel are the main learning points from Chapter 4?	Elaborate on why you feel these points are key.

Notes

1. For further information, contact Zenger–Miller, 1735 Technology Drive, San Jose, CA 95110.

2. A. Jay, "How to Run a Meeting," *Harvard Business Review* 54(2) (March–April 1976): p. 47.

3. H. O'Neill, "How to Run Meetings—and How Not To," *Management Today,* March 1982, p. 44.

4. C. Hymowitz, "A Survival Guide to the Office Meeting," *The Wall Street Journal,* June 21, 1988, p. 41.

5. G. W. Soden, "Avoid Meetings or Make Them Work," *Business Horizons* 27(2) (March–April 1984): p. 48.

6. L. Oppenheim, *Making Meetings Matter: A Report to the 3M Corporation* (Philadelphia, Wharton Center for Applied Research, 1987), p. 21.

7. A. Bartlett, personal communication.

CHAPTER FIVE

PLANNING THE PROCESS OF A SESSION TO MINE GROUP GOLD: THREE PHASES TO SUCCESS

CHAPTER OBJECTIVES

➤ To demonstrate the vital role that *process* plays in the success of a group session.

➤ To provide practical strategies for using simple, but powerful processes to achieve a session's purpose and outcomes.

INTRODUCTION

Having planned the structure you must now plan the session's process. The question is: "What set of activities should be employed to maximize the group's ability to achieve the session's purpose and desired outcomes?" Raudsepp recalls an incident on a golf course that demonstrates the value of a good process in achieving desired outcomes.

It was the 16th hole in the annual Bob Hope Desert Classic, and the tall, handsome newcomer had an excellent chance of winning. His iron shot fell just short of the green, giving him a good chance for a birdie. Smiling broadly, he strode down the fairway only to stop in dismay. His ball had rolled into a brown paper bag carelessly tossed on the ground by someone in the gallery. If he removed the ball from the bag, it would cost him a penalty stroke. If he tried to hit the ball and the bag, he would lose control over the shot. For a moment he pondered the problem. Then he solved it.[1]

Assuming the desired outcome in this situation is to cleanly hit the ball without losing a penalty stroke, what process would enable that? The answer: set fire to the bag. The day was saved. A creative, simple process turned a particularly troublesome situation into a productive one.

Process is crucial to successful task completion within group sessions. Don't sell it short; take time to plan your process. Countless group sessions have been wasted because a poorly conceived process—akin to trying to hit the golf ball while it was in the bag—unraveled in the middle of the meeting, control of the session was lost, and there was no way to recover.

The crucial factor in developing any group process is to keep it as streamlined as possible. Let its elegance be rooted in its creativity and simplicity, not its complexity. A well-planned process will ease the facilitation task because the process itself will preempt some of the pitfalls and negative situations that might otherwise occur during a group session.

The tips, ideas, and techniques presented here are valuable to anyone planning the process part of a group session. The techniques are categorized by meeting stage (beginning, middle, and end); they are field-tested; they are uncomplicated; they are easy to facilitate; and, best of all, they are effective in moving a group toward goal achievement. These processes show you how to "set your paper bag on fire."

THE START OF A GROUP SESSION: GETTING PEOPLE INVOLVED

Excellent meetings almost universally have excellent beginnings. The climate and mood that transcends the entire session typically is established during the first fifteen to twenty minutes. Beginnings must never be taken for granted or disregarded as some worthless rite of passage that the meeting leader must tolerate until getting down to the real business at hand.

The beginning sets the tone. It can help make people feel good about attending because the setting is warm and inviting, or it can make people feel turned off because the opening is disorganized, cold, and unfriendly. A flexible beginning, one that integrates people into the session as they arrive rather than having some wait for others, gives a positive boost to people's initial attitudes about the session. There are a number of ways to kick off a session; four processes (serving four different requirements) are presented here.

Informal Warm-up Period

Acknowledge the need for a social warm-up period and allow for it by posting five to ten minutes against it on the agenda. A warmup is going to take place whether or not you have scheduled one, so it is best to "go with the flow" and plan for it.

An informal warm-up is especially important for staff meetings and other group sessions where everyone knows everyone else. The informal discussions and joking that precede many sessions may appear to be extraneous or a waste of time; in fact, these periods are invaluable as they serve to create a relaxed atmosphere. Five or ten minutes of informality leading off the session encourages a release of tension, allows business to be transacted, gives people time to collect their thoughts before beginning, and gets the small talk out of the way.

In order for the informal warm-up process to be effective, you and your group members need to discuss its intent. Shared values need to be built so that everyone views the warm-up as a legitimate part of every agenda.

Under no circumstances should the informal warm-up be taken as a license to come to the session five, ten, or fifteen minutes late. The ground rule must be: "our meetings will start promptly at the scheduled time, everyone is expected to be on time, and the first item on the agenda is a short, informal, social warm-up."

Welcoming Sheet

A more structured opening process can be orchestrated by using a welcoming sheet—a flip chart page or large piece of cardboard that contains both a greeting and beginning instructions for the arrivals. Make sure the welcoming sheet is strategically placed so the meeting participants can't miss it once inside the room. Exhibit 5–1 shows an example of a welcoming sheet.

EXHIBIT 5–1: WELCOMING SHEET

WELCOME
AND
GOOD MORNING!

PLEASE HELP YOURSELF TO A DANISH
AND COFFEE, TEA, OR JUICE.

DO NOT SIT DOWN. CIRCULATE!

INTRODUCE YOURSELF
TO AT LEAST FIVE OTHER PEOPLE.
TELL THEM A LITTLE BIT
ABOUT YOURSELF AND
SHARE WITH THEM WHAT
YOU HOPE TO GET OUT OF THIS SESSION.

WE WILL CONCLUDE THIS ACTIVITY
BY 8:15

Paired Interviews

This process is particularly productive when most people at the session will be strangers. As soon as people start to arrive, ask them verbally, or by a welcoming sheet, to find a partner to interview. Hand each person a sheet of paper containing a set of interview questions. The pairs proceed to interview each other and record each other's responses on the sheet provided.

There should be no more than six or seven questions, and at least half of them should have some direct tie to the purpose of the session. The questions can vary from the thought-provoking to the light-hearted. The following examples illustrate the types of questions that might be asked.

➤ What is your name, organization, and job title?

➤ What kind of work do you do?

➤ In your present position, what has been the toughest challenge you have faced?

➤ What are the main forces (internal or external) boosting the competitive edge of your company in the marketplace; what are the main forces hindering its competitive edge?

➤ What can you personally do to help your department become more effective?

➤ What are the three most vivid memories you have from your childhood?

➤ If you had a one-year sabbatical, what would you do with your time? Why?

➤ If you were the head of your department or group, what changes would you implement? Why?

When the interviews are finished, the sheets are exchanged so that each person has his or her own data. The participants then circulate and meet others by sharing the information on their sheets.

Name Card Collage

If seating is not to be preassigned, have available a variety of colored paper, magazines, scissors, markers, tape, etc., and encourage people to make a "name card collage" that best represents them as a person. When finished, have each participant explain the meaning behind their creation. This is a simple but energizing beginning.

The ideas presented here are just the tip of the iceberg; you can probably think of many others. In planning the process for getting started, the key is to create an activity that encourages open and nonthreatening interaction among all participants prior to settling down to the task(s) at hand. A good beginning rarely happens; it requires thoughtful planning. Getting off to a good start provides initial momentum for a productive session.

THE HEART OF A GROUP SESSION: SHARING AND PROCESSING GROUP INFORMATION

The middle of a group session is where the bulk of the work is carried out. The trick for the session planner at this stage is to plan a process, or set of processes, that will prompt the group members to share their thoughts, feelings, ideas, and data, and ensure that this information is treated in an organized manner.

Often the sharing and processing of information can be handled in close sequence, as is the case with brainstorming, certain subgroup activities, and force field analysis.

For example, with brainstorming, ideas are shared in a totally uninhibited environment that is free from criticism. Immediately after all ideas have been shared, the group processes the information that has been generated by discussing, refining, modifying, and eliminating items.

With force field analysis, a list of the positive, driving forces involved in a change situation is created, as is a list of negative, restraining forces. Once the information-sharing phase is finished, the group goes on to information processing by reviewing, modifying, and eliminating forces on both lists and weighting the remaining ones according to relative strengths. Processing continues by developing a strategy that will maximize the driving forces and minimize the restraining forces.

Just as there are many options for opening a group session, there are many methods and techniques for developing and acting upon information during the middle portion of the session. After gaining experience and confidence in using some of the ideas suggested below, feel free to refine these to meet your own needs or to create other, similar processes.

The approaches provided here are particularly applicable in a wide variety of group situations: staff meetings, problem-solving sessions, communications meetings, task forces, strategy development sessions, and the like.

Structured Pre-Work

Taking advantage of structured pre-work is one of the simplest and quickest ways that you can focus the group's energies on the topics of greatest concern. When planned and implemented properly, this strategy increases efficiency by eliminating a significant amount of the time wasted as group members attempt to read, comprehend, and react to material they are seeing for the first time.

Given the typical situation of new or freshly revised material, complex issues within the material, and tight time constraints in the session, it is extremely difficult for the group to effectively work on the issues.

The attractiveness of the structured pre-work process is that the burden for reading, comprehending, and developing initial reactions to the material is shifted to each individual outside of the session; this, in turn, frees precious meeting time for the group to do what it needs to do most—process the information together.

What are the most critical factors to consider when using the structured pre-work technique?

Give Adequate Lead Time.   Whoever assigns pre-work must ensure that it reaches the participants with enough lead time for them to thoroughly digest the content before the group session. This lead time can be anywhere from a few days to a month or more, depending on the complexity of the material and what activities are required.

Provide Clear Pre-Work Instructions. It is imperative that the participants be given clear instructions as to what they are expected to do with the material before the session. Here are some examples:

➤ Read the attached report thoroughly and be prepared to discuss the pros and cons of the ideas presented.

➤ Analyze the attached data and formulate your position regarding the proposed design change. All unit members will be given five minutes to present their initial position to the whole group.

➤ Read the results of the District Restructuring Study and respond to the four questions that are attached at the end. We will discuss all four in detail.

➤ Revise the attached budget figures in light of your new objectives and be prepared to discuss your rationale for any changes. Based on your inputs and our discussion, I will formulate a revised budget for the team to consider at our May 20 session.

Emphasize the Need to Complete Pre-Work. When developing the instructions, be sure to emphasize that incomplete pre-work will impair the information processing activity planned during the upcoming session. After sending out your pre-work, a personal follow-up—a quick phone call or e-mail note—sends a powerful message that you are serious about attendees coming prepared. You'll be pleasantly surprised at the results your little reinforcement message will bring.

Assign Pre-Work Only If It Will Be Used. After emphasizing the importance of coming to the session properly prepared, you must then make use of the data the participants have generated or risk losing credibility. Also, an effective tool like structured pre-work will be rendered useless when participants begin to realize that they can save personal time and effort by ignoring your pre-work requests because you rarely use the information you asked for.

Plan the Process for In-Session Use of Pre-Work. The manner in which the pre-work will be handled in the session is a critical planning consideration. Techniques described later in this section (present, then discuss; buzz groups; small work groups; introspection, then share) will furnish practical ideas for working through the pre-work material.

Selectively employing pre-work advances the productivity of the group session. The participants come to the session with a deeper insight into the topic(s). Having had time to think about and organize their initial thoughts, feelings, and ideas, the group is primed to spend its time really working the issues rather than "flailing to understand them."

Getting the Most from Presentations

One often used, and definitely most abused, meeting process is the presentation/discussion. Typically, the process goes something like this:

Suzanne starts to present her information; five minutes into her presentation, she is interrupted; several other group members chime in; the whole group gets sidetracked and moves into a phase variously described as "group grope," "random walk," or "dance in a dark room."

Ten or fifteen minutes are wasted as Suzanne attempts to regain control of the session. She speaks for another five minutes, is interrupted, and the cycle starts all over again.

In this typical scenario, a 45-minute agenda item—15 minutes of presentation followed by 30 minutes of discussion—is extended to two hours of chaos and frustration. Little or nothing is resolved and the group ends up 75 minutes behind schedule.

This brief drama depicts the debilitating group process that meeting participants often encounter. All is not lost, however. By taking into account the following planning considerations, presentations can be transformed into a potent group process.

Keep Presentations Separate from Discussion. Disciplined facilitation, which ensures that the presentation phase is completed before the debate and discussion phase is allowed to begin, is the cornerstone of success for this process. If the presentation is to last 30 minutes or more, talk to the presenter beforehand and see if he or she can't divide the talk into 15- or 20-minute blocks. Have the presenter give the first block, then open group discussion. Follow with the second block, then discussion; continue with as many blocks as necessary.

Allow Only Clarification During the Presentation. During the presentation phase, questions of clarification can be asked (in fact, they should be encouraged) to make certain that people are listening to and grasping the information being presented. But don't allow questions to develop into a discussion of the material being presented until the presentation is complete.

Develop a Set of Focused Discussion Areas. Before the session at which the presentation will be given, you should do two things:

1. Make certain that the presentation is relevant to the needs of your group, and, if it is, communicate this to the members ahead of time so they have a general idea about the thrust of the presentation.

2. In conjunction with your group, develop three to six discussion areas that will be the focal points for the discussion portion after the presentation.

Advance planning will help ensure that the group members extract the most meaning from the upcoming presentation. The focus areas generated by the group members prior to the presentation will pinpoint the areas most pertinent to their needs. Whenever possible, informing the presenter of the focus areas ahead of time is necessary because it defines audience expectations and gives the presenter the opportunity to meet these expectations by shaping the presentation accordingly. Examples of possible focused discussion areas, for note-taking during the presentation and for guiding group dialogue at the conclusion of the presentation, include:

> ➤ What points in the presentation do we agree with or support?

> ➤ What points in the presentation do we disagree with or not support? Why?

> ➤ How can our group take maximum advantage of the idea being proposed?

> ➤ What experiences can we recall that would amplify or illustrate the theme of the presentation?

> ➤ What procedures can we put in place to resolve the issue presented?

> ➤ What is the impact of the proposed action for our group?

> ➤ Based on the information presented, what should be our next step?

Facilitate the Two Phases.   The mechanisms for facilitating the present, then discuss phases are straightforward. Before introducing the presenter, distribute the list of focused discussion areas and ask the group to make brief notes for each of the areas as they listen.

After the presentation, the whole group—with the presenter included as a team member—explores the focused discussion areas one at a time.

Used in the manner described, the present, then discuss approach becomes an excellent group process tool. There is forethought given to what the group wants from the presentation; there is a disciplined flow that avoids interruption, sidetracking, showboating, etc.; people are actively involved during the presentation by asking clarifying questions and/or by taking notes; participants are more active in the post-presentation discussion because they have collected their thoughts on paper; and the presenter—by being asked to sit down at the table with the group—is psychologically made to feel like an ally during the discussion rather than an outsider or an adversary.

Two Cases of Presentation Facilitation

The following experiences of Carin, assistant vice president of strategic planning for a financial services company, provides wonderful insight into the facilitation of presentations. Carin's company needed to close two of its 24 district offices, one in the Gulf Coast Region and one in the Great Lakes Region. She developed a presentation for each regional staff which included the region vice president, the six district managers and the three regional HQ staff members.

Presentation to the Gulf Coast Region.   During her presentation to the Gulf Coast Region, Carin made a compelling case for closing a particular district office. She had marshaled her facts, involved the six district managers in the data collection, and made a solid analysis. However, her presentation and corresponding staff decision-making time, scheduled for one hour, turned into a two hour "slugfest." She said later that it was like being in front of a firing squad. It was a classic case of "killing the messenger bearing bad news."

The presentation started out well enough, but Carin gradually became the focal point for the group's frustration for having to close an office. The staff started picking her numbers apart even though they had been heavily involved in generating them. From her individual discussions, she knew her recommendations had the blessing of some people; but, they were not speaking up. In fact, she had counted on the region vice president and one particular district manager for additional strategic arguments to support her case. Instead, they jumped on the bandwagon with the vocal dominators. After the two hours of parrying and thrusting, the staff did reach a decision: Send Carin back for more information and postpone making a final decision on which office to close until next month's staff meeting.

Presentation to the Great Lakes Region.   Carin had to make the same general presentation to the Great Lakes Regional staff. Only this time it was different. That vice president, having learned the principles of *Mining Group Gold*, planned an agenda using the "present, then discuss" approach. Because the staff members had been involved in providing data and assumptions—just like the Gulf Coast staff—everyone had good insight into the direction Carin's presentation was going to take. The Great Lakes Region staff prepared a set of focused discussion questions to insure a thorough discussion of her material.

Carin presented everything in 15 minutes including time for several interruptions regarding questions of clarification. When finished, the vice president invited her to sit down at the table and "join us in a constructive debate on the recommendations from your fine presentation." Carin was out of the "line of fire." And, even though the debate got heated, the vice president's primary facilitation—and the staff members' secondary facilitation—kept everything under control. Being looked upon as a collaborative member of the staff, Carin felt comfortable relaying adversarial questions over to the staff members she knew supported her. This helped make the thoughts of others apparent, enriched the discussion, and brought forth a balanced perspective.

Within 45 minutes the staff reached a consensus to support Carin's general recommendations with a few modifications. What had taken two hours with no final decision at Gulf Coast, had taken one hour and resulted in a consensus decision at Great Lakes. While everything remained on hold and uncertain in the Gulf Coast Region, the Great Lakes Region immediately sprang into action taking the necessary steps to close the office. People were not left to wonder about their fate and spread more rumors for another month.

In-Session Subgrouping

Any time the group consists of 10 or more, you will need to give serious consideration to using subgroups for part or all of the meeting. Facilitation complications multiply tremendously at this size and over.

Breaking a whole group into several small groups and providing a basic structure to help them simultaneously process their assigned task(s) is an underused technique. Many groups get caught in the rut of working on every agenda item as a whole group. Not only is this unnecessary, it is impractical and ineffective.

A great deal of synergy and productivity can be captured with a well-conceived subgroup process. The large group meeting takes on the qualities of a small group meeting. From a planning perspective, the following points are important.

Determine Space Requirements.   If possible, subgroups that are going to spend several hours working intensely on a task should have the convenience of a breakout room that provides privacy and comfort. In determining the number of breakout rooms required, keep in mind that the main meeting room can double as one of the breakout rooms.

With shorter activities, however, unless the facility is unduly small, having the subgroups stay in the main meeting room and congregate in the corners of the room (or at each end of the table) is usually very productive. The hum that permeates the room is energizing, there is an air of participation and involvement, and the manager can join a subgroup as an active member while still being available to move from group to group to lend assistance where needed.

Decide on Subgroup Size.   The dynamics of group interaction change dramatically depending on how big the group is. The guidelines that follow will give an idea of the interactions between members of different-sized groups.

➤ **Twos.** Not really a subgroup because there are not enough members. However, dividing people into pairs and having them carry out an assigned task one-on-one is a way to maximize group interaction. As described earlier, pairs often are used during a get-acquainted period or when there is a need to get everyone immediately involved.

➤ **Threes.** The barest minimum that forms a subgroup. Intimate, everyone can get involved. When members meet in trios to discuss a topic and prepare either a report on their discussion, or questions to be offered to the total group, two purposes are served: (1) everyone has a chance to speak; and (2) a degree of anonymity is preserved, since the report or questions comes from three people rather than from an individual. As a consequence, greater depth or intensity is often achieved. The one danger with a group of three is that one member can dominate the other two.

➤ **Fours.** Reasonably effective. Dividing a group into subgroups of four can be useful for obtaining a sense of the meeting by getting a quick reading on attitudes and reactions within the subgroups before coming to a whole group decision. Domination by one member is also a risk in a group of this size.

➤ **Fives and Sixes.** A subgroup of five or six is ideal for working on a task. Best results usually are achieved from subgroups of this size. The physical closeness and eye contact aid in communication. Diverse perspectives, supported by a mix of ideas, opinions, and attitudes promotes creative thinking.

➤ **Sevens.** Quite effective but starting to get a little large.

➤ **Eights and Nines.** The internal structure really starts to break down in subgroups of this size. Coalitions or side conversations often occur. Although results are usually satisfactory, the time to get these results is longer than with subgroups of five or six.

➤ **Tens or More.** Very unsatisfactory as a subgroup unless there is a desire to illustrate the interaction problems of groups. Using ten or more individuals can be effective for demonstrating how group participants can get in each other's way and negatively affect group accomplishments.

Figure the Composition of Subgroups. Composition will vary depending on the objectives of the specific task. Unless there is a need to do otherwise, the rule of thumb is to make each subgroup a microcosm of the whole group in terms of diversity of experience, knowledge, skills, abilities, etc. For some situations, loading a particular subgroup with people possessing the same strength may be appropriate.

Assessing the potential chemistry within each subgroup is also critical. The considerations outlined in Chapter 4 regarding the chemistry of the group on a macro level are just as relevant for the subgroup on a micro level. For instance, depending on the specific objectives, placing two people together who do not get along may, or may not, be a good idea.

Planning the subgroup activity itself requires three phases:

1. What should transpire within each subgroup during the simultaneous work sessions.

2. What supplies and materials are required to complete the assigned subgroup activity.

3. How should the whole group operate when sharing and integrating the outputs of the subgroups.

Develop the Subgroup Activity. The following paragraphs describe several small-group activities and the type of results to be expected.

One method of stimulating group effort is the *buzz group*. In teams of three to five, people are asked to interact—to "buzz"—for a short period of time (usually not more than 10 to 15 minutes) in response to an instruction such as, "Generate a set of pros and cons to the draft of the new absenteeism policy that I just covered. Be prepared to share your reactions with the whole group in ten minutes."

Small work groups—teams with five to seven members— are larger than buzz groups, they are given more complicated tasks to perform, and they are given more time to perform them—from 30 minutes to several hours. Assuming three small work groups, the plan can be to assign the same task to all three groups. For example, "Brainstorm, consolidate, and prioritize a list of behaviors a good facilitator practices in facilitating a group."

A variation to this approach is to assign each of the three subgroups a different task to pursue. For example, "Team A is to develop a force field analysis on the forces driving the successful implementation of staff development within our hospital and those hindering its successful implementation. Team B is to develop a process for objectively evaluating the worth of a potential staff development workshop to our hospital. Team C will create a fair method for selecting who gets to attend which staff development workshops during the next calendar year."

With either buzz activities or small work group activities, Maier suggests, "If a specific number of ideas is required, the number of ideas to be reported by each subgroup should be fewer than the number of people in it. This prevents the group product from being a simple compilation of the contributions made by each member. Good information processing requires the resolution of differences, and one way to introduce such differences is to require the group to be selective and integrative rather than additive."[2]

Determine what supplies and materials are required to complete the subgroup activity and ensure their availability to each subgroup when needed. At a minimum, you will need to provide a flip chart stand and paper, water color markers (dark colors like black, purple, blue, brown), and drafting tape.

Develop the Whole-Group Process to Be Used When the Subgroup Activity is Completed. Once the subgroup work is completed, there is a need for each subgroup to feed back to the whole group the output of its efforts. There are a variety of ways to do this, including the following:

➤ The larger group reconvenes; each subgroup shares its top two ideas or highest priority items. After each subgroup has had a chance to do this, the lower-priority ideas or items can be added.

➤ Each subgroup writes its report on flip chart paper and hangs it on the wall for everyone to review. This makes for a useful interlude since, in addition to stretching and reading, people can pick up a cup of coffee, leave the room briefly, or get immediate clarification on points of confusion.

➤ Short, stand-up presentations are made by each subgroup. As each is made, the scribe records the main points on a flip chart for the benefit of the whole group.

➤ If there is easy access to a copier, copies are made of each subgroup's report. This information is then distributed to every participant, discussed, and key points are consolidated on flip chart paper.

➤ Each subgroup gives its reports to a central processing team. The team condenses and synthesizes the results and communicates its findings later in the same session or at the next session.

When planning the whole-group process, keep the sharing and processing activities streamlined yet interesting for everyone. Try to maximize the number of people involved in the whole-group processing activity. The previous examples illustrate a number of ways to do this.

During the information sharing, the facilitator must focus on clarification and testing comprehension to make certain everyone understands what is being presented.

During the processing portion, the facilitator works with the whole group to develop a summary that highlights the main points addressed during the general presentations. A good scribe will be a big help during this phase.

Subgroup activities are not idle exercises; therefore, managing the sharing and processing of information at the whole-group level requires careful thought. A poor whole-group plan can ruin terrific work at the subgroup level.

Introspection, Then Sharing

An alternative to asking a difficult question and then having group members immediately launch into a discussion is to have the participants do some silent reflecting first. The purpose is to give everyone time to mentally process a particular item, to gain personal insight, and to assess how others might feel before conferring about the issue. This individual preparation prior to interacting with others will invigorate the initial group dialogue because people will be primed to interact.

Two generic questions that always prove to be stimulating during the introspection phase are: "What are the pluses and minuses to the position you are taking?" and "Who are the people and/or groups that might support, question, or reject your position? What would they say to you about your stance?"

These basic questions can be used in any situation where it is important that the participants crystallize the rationale for their position and make an assessment of how others might react to it before discussing and debating the issue in a group.

Introspection, then sharing, is an elementary process that invariably produces a dynamic group discussion.

Conclude Along the Way

Don't wait until the session's wrap-up to summarize and generate conclusions for the first time. The productivity of a group session can be increased if the manager, working from the facilitator's role, helps the group reach conclusions throughout the session.

The task behavior of summarizing is an activity that should be performed repeatedly as progress is made through the agenda. Developing summarizing conclusions along the way is important because it keeps the discussion focused. Summarizing cuts down on confusion and on the tendency to wander off into irrelevancies. Also, if you wait until the end of the session to summarize everything, the sheer volume of information processed during most meetings makes developing meaningful conclusions very difficult, if not impossible. You should facilitate a conclusion:

➤ After each topic, agenda item, or task is brought to a close.

➤ Periodically as a long and complex topic is being addressed.

➤ Any time there is a question about what has been decided.

➤ Just before a decision is to be made, to set the stage for the decision-making process.

➤ Just after the decision is made, to ensure everyone's understanding of the decision or outcome.

The method for facilitating a conclusion will vary depending on the topic and desired outcome. A few suggestions for managing the periodic conclusion process are:

➤ The person responsible for the minutes can be asked to read aloud his or her notes regarding the item or task just finished. Check this with the group to make sure everyone is in accord.

➤ A volunteer from the group can be asked to provide his or her thoughts about the topic's conclusion. Ask the rest of the group if it agrees.

➤ Acting as a facilitator, state your sense of the discussion and the conclusions reached. Ask group members if they concur.

The final conclusion for that agenda item should be written on a flip chart by the scribe, checked with the group to make sure the wording is correct and complete, and posted on the wall for later reference.

THE END OF A GROUP SESSION: FINISHING WITH SNAP

At this stage in the planning sequence, you must determine the means for ending the session so that there are no loose ends. People need to leave knowing what was accomplished, what remains to be accomplished, what happens next, and "what we did well" and "not so well" from a process standpoint.

There are four tasks that need to be planned to make certain that the group session finishes with power and impact as opposed to drifting off into oblivion. Remember, the close of one meeting is often the first step in preparing for the next.

Take Care of Any "Leftovers"

Any agenda items scheduled but not covered, or tasks started but not fully completed, need to be dealt with. This can be accomplished by:

➤ Adding them to the next session's agenda.

➤ Delegating certain items to subgroups or individuals to pursue outside of the session with results reported at a future date.

➤ Tabling for a later time (beyond the next session).

➤ Dropping the item altogether.

Review the Outcomes

Using the flip charts developed earlier that contain the conclusions for each item covered, review any decisions reached during the session and reemphasizes the "who is to do what by when" action items. For example:

"Regarding our third action item, Lisa, you've committed to pulling together two exempts and two non-exempts from our department to design our display for this year's American Software Convention. Also, you've agreed to have a first sketch of the display for us to review on June 23, two weeks from today. Right?"

The "right" at the end tests comprehension to ensure that you and Lisa see the action item the same way. If there are differences regarding what was agreed to, these issues can be brought up and resolved now, or soon after the session.

Highlight Items for Next Session

The next session "strawman agenda" is established by noting any items to be carried over from the current session, plus any new topics proposed for next time. For example:

You might state, "So, the one item we will carry over from today's session and include on our next agenda is Strickland's replacement. The three desired outcomes will remain the same: list of potential replacements developed, all candidates on the list discussed, and interview list of top three candidates determined." The scribe writes this information on a flip chart under the heading, Next Session.

"Does anyone have any new topics to propose for next time? Yes, Desmond."

"We need to process the new Customer Relations Workshop for our tellers. The desired outcome should be: workshop implementation schedule covering all 36 branches agreed-to."

Hold a Session Critique

George Santayana, Spanish poet and philosopher, made an observation about history that relates to meeting assessment: "Those who cannot remember the past are condemned to repeat it." So it is with meetings.

A 5- to 10-minute critique of the entire session, in order to remember the past, is a must if a group is serious about improving its meeting process. Oppenheim, citing research conducted by the Wharton Center for Applied Research, emphatically underscores this point.

> A set of skills that are valued in organizations which take meetings seriously involve eliciting and providing feedback about the meeting itself. Many of the tasks we carry out provide feedback to us about their satisfactory completion, and meetings should be no exception. Many managers, when asked, say they can tell if a meeting was good or bad. Unfortunately, "good" and "bad" are often global evaluations from which we learn very little. They may have less to do with what went on in the meeting than what goes on in the organizational context. Feedback about key aspects of the meeting could, if legitimized, stimulate very powerful discussions that would improve productivity within the meeting room and beyond.[3]

There are various ways to hold a meaningful session critique.

Open Discussion.   A very simple but effective technique is for the manager to draw a line down the center of a flip chart page and label the columns as indicated in Exhibit 5–2 (the $\triangle$ is the symbol for change). The manager solicits and records the points offered by the group—including his or her own—with respect to both questions. The group then reaches a consensus on one or two items from the "do better" side that it most wants to improve next time. The group also concurs on an item from the left side that it would like to continue "doing well." These items are circled. The data from this flip chart page is included in the minutes so the "do betters" for next time are documented, and a running record that tracks session improvement is preserved.

The two areas for improvement and the activity to continue doing well should be reviewed first thing at the next meeting by the manager. This will refresh everyone's memory about the session's meeting improvement goals and will demonstrate that the manager is serious about enhancing group session productivity and teamwork.

A few words of caution about the open discussion critique. This is a serious exercise. While environmental considerations may be important, and may require improvements if the team must continue meeting in the same place, the manager cannot allow the chart to constantly fill up with things like: the room

Exhibit 5–2: MEETING ASSESSMENT RESULTS FROM OPEN DISCUSSION

+ What did we do well today? +	△ What could we do better next time? △
Had desired outcomes for each agenda topic	Shared facilitation; we all need to help Cal more—a successful session is not just his responsibility, it's everyones'
Excellent timekeeping by Tina	
Primary facilitator (Cal) concluded along the way	Have supplies and materials on hand; Maria had to leave halfway through the session and go searching for markers and tape
Used subgoups effectively during assessment activity	
Team made conscious decision to extend agenda time on item 3 and drop item 5	Start on time; not 15 minutes late
	Test comprehension in complex discussions (like vacation shutdown) to avoid confusion
—	Howard and Gary need to do pre-work
—	
etc.	—
	—
	etc.

was too hot; the donuts were delicious; the coffee was cold; the view was terrific; the chairs were uncomfortable; the carpet was dirty; and, Dan's shirt was pretty. These items don't hit at the things that are going to make for a stronger, more collaborative team. Also, the manager has to facilitate against meaningless, round-worded statements like: we had lots of good discussion; the agenda wasn't any good; this was an outstanding session; there was too much arguing; we got quite a bit accomplished; and, we need more structure. If this starts to occur, ask the respondent to elaborate. "What, specifically, pleased you about the discussion?" Or, "In what aspects of our session do we need more structure?"

The open discussion method requires organized thinking to make it a meaningful session improvement technique. In general, the team will do well to provide direct, specific feedback in these major categories: pre-planning; pre-work; in-session structure, processes, teamwork, and facilitation; and, action item follow-up.

Session Survey. A second alternative involves handing out a short survey form that contains a series of meeting dimensions. The participants rate the session's effectiveness on these dimensions and then pass their completed form to the minute taker. This person will consolidate the rating results outside the session and publish them in the minutes.

As with the open discussion method, documenting the session evaluation in the minutes furnishes a history of the group's progress of improvement against selected dimensions.

The Discussion Assessment Survey (Exhibit 5–3) is a simple form comprised of eight dimensions that focus on group interaction. The Group Session Effectiveness Evaluation (Exhibit 5–4) is a basic instrument containing 16 dimensions covering both the structural and interactive aspects of group sessions. The chapter summary and Notes Worksheet conclude Chapter 5.

With proper planning of the meeting's structure and process now completed, well begun is half done. The next stage is implementation. Chapters 6, 7, and 8 furnish tools and ideas aimed at increasing the manager's confidence and ability to facilitate the group in achieving the session's overall purpose and desired outcomes.

Exhibit 5–3: DISCUSSION ASSESSMENT SURVEY

Session's

Title _____ Date _____ Time _____

Clarity of direction

1. Most of us were confused about the purpose and desired outcomes of this session.
   1 2 3 4 5
   We all understood the purpose and desired outcomes of this session.

Structure

2. Our discussion went in several directions at once.
   1 2 3 4 5
   Our discussion was orderly; no ideas were lost in the shuffle.

Flow

3. Our discussion required a great deal of back-tracking and reorienting.
   1 2 3 4 5
   Our discussion moved forward with succeeding points building on previous ones.

Participation

4. Some dominated the discussion while others contributed much less.
   1 2 3 4 5
   We all shared the floor in this discussion.

Expression of differences

5. Our disagreeing produced defensive reactions.
   1 2 3 4 5
   We disagreed without arousing defensive reactions.

Listening

6. We didn't listen to each other very well.
   1 2 3 4 5
   We demonstrated that we were listening to each other.

Understanding

7. Most of us were confused about what went on in this discussion.
   1 2 3 4 5
   We all understood what was discussed and agreed to.

Achievement of session's desired outcomes

8. We cannot tell if desired outcomes were achieved because they were not stated or were confused. *OR,* if stated, we failed to achieve them.
   1 2 3 4 5
   We fully achieved the desired outcomes set forth and clarified for this session.

Exhibit 5–4: GROUP SESSION EFFECTIVENESS EVALUATION

Session's
    Title _____ Date _____ Time _____

1. Were you notified of this session in time to make arrangements and sufficiently prepare for it?

1	2	3	4	5

It was last minute   Time to minimally   Yes, plenty of time
No time to prepare   prepare   to fully prepare

2. Were the session's key particulars (who was calling the meeting, where it would be held, when it would start, when it would end, and who was invited) clearly communicated in advance?

1	2	3	4	5

No, not   Stated   Yes, clearly stated
communicated, had   but unclear   in writing, in
to track down   advance of the
myself   session

3. Was the session's purpose clearly stated?

1	2	3	4	5

Not stated   Stated,   Clearly stated, plus
                           but vague   posted in the session

4. Were the session's desired outcomes clearly stated?

1	2	3	4	5

Not stated   Stated,   Clearly stated, plus
                           but vague   posted in the session.

5. Was either a predetermined agenda reviewed, or an in-session agenda created, at the beginning of the session?

1	2	3	4	5

Not stated   Vague agenda   Specified agenda

Exhibit 5–4: GROUP SESSION EFFECTIVENESS EVALUATION
(Continued)

---

6. Were roles (primary facilitator, minute taker, timekeeper, flip chart scribe, etc.) defined and assigned at the beginning of the session?

```
1              2              3              4              5
└──────────────┴──────────────┴──────────────┴──────────────┘
```

Not discussed, defined, or assigned	Alluded to, not specifically defined or assigned	Clearly defined, assigned, and posted in the session

7. As the session progressed, was the agenda "managed" by revisiting and modifying: the number of topics; their order; their desired outcomes; and their time-frames based on changing circumstances within the session?

```
1              2              3              4              5
└──────────────┴──────────────┴──────────────┴──────────────┘
```

No, inflexible agenda rigidly adhered to despite need to modify	Somewhat flexible agenda, modified with reluctance	Yes, flexible agenda modified if and when required

8. Were all action items relative to "who is to do what by when" clearly stated before the session adjourned?

```
1              2              3              4              5
└──────────────┴──────────────┴──────────────┴──────────────┘
```

Not stated	Stated, but vague	Clearly stated

9. To what extent were we able to achieve our desired outcomes?

```
1              2              3              4              5
└──────────────┴──────────────┴──────────────┴──────────────┘
```

Don't know because none were stated -OR- (If desired outcomes were stated) we failed to achieve them	Partially achieved	Fully achieved

10. Was the information that was shared and processed during this session useful to you?

```
1              2              3              4              5
└──────────────┴──────────────┴──────────────┴──────────────┘
```

Not at all useful	Somewhat useful	All of it was useful

Exhibit 5–4: GROUP SESSION EFFECTIVENESS EVALUATION
(Concluded)

11. Were you comfortable in asking questions?

1	2	3	4	5

Not at all
comfortable

Moderately
comfortable

Totally comfortable

12. Were you satisfied that your questions were answered openly and honestly?

1	2	3	4	5

Very dissatisfied

Neither satisfied
or dissatisfied

Very
satisfied

13. Were you satisfied with the group's functioning relative to teamwork and cooperation?

1	2	3	4	5

Very dissatisfied

Neither satisfied
or dissatisfied

Very satisfied

14. To what extent do you feel your participation influenced the group's ability to achieve its desired outcome(s)?

1	2	3	4	5

No influence at all

Moderate influence

A great deal of
influence

15. To what extent were your ideas/positions understood by the other participants?

1	2	3	4	5

Not at all
understood

Somewhat
understood

Completely
understood

16. To what extent were the ideas/positions of the other participants understood by you?

1	2	3	4	5

Not at all
understood

Somewhat
understood

Completely
understood

CHAPTER FIVE SUMMARY

THE START OF A GROUP SESSION: GETTING PEOPLE INVOLVED

Informal Warmup Period
Welcoming Sheet
Paired Interviews
Name Card Collage

THE HEART OF A GROUP SESSION: SHARING AND PROCESSING GROUP INFORMATION

Structured Pre-Work
- Give adequate lead time
- Provide clear pre-work instructions
- Emphasize the need to complete pre-work
- Assign pre-work only if it will be used
- Plan the process for the in-session use of pre work

Getting the Most From Presentations
- Keep presentations separate from discussion
- Allow only clarification during the presentation
- Develop a set of focused discussion areas
- Facilitate the "present" and the "discuss" phases

In-Session Subgrouping
- Determine space requirements
- Decide on subgroup size
- Figure the composition of subgroups
- Develop the subgroup activity
- Develop the whole-group process to be used when the subgroup activity is completed

Introspection, Then Sharing
Conclude Along the Way

THE END OF A GROUP SESSION: FINISHING WITH SNAP

Take Care of Any "Leftovers"
Review the Outcomes
Highlight Items for Next Session
Hold a Session Critique
- Open discussion
- Session Survey

Notes Worksheet: DEVELOP WRITTEN RESPONSES TO THE TWO
ITEMS LISTED BELOW

What do you feel are the main learning points from Chapter 5?	Elaborate on why you feel these points are key.

Notes

1. E. Raudsepp, "Are You a Creative Executive?" *Management Review,* February 1978, p. 12.

2. N. R. F. Maier, *Psychology in Industry,* 3d ed. (Boston: Houghton Mifflin, 1965), p. 20.

3. L. Oppenheim, *Making Meetings Matter: A Report to the 3M Corporation* (Philadelphia: Wharton Center for Applied Research, 1987), p. 38.

CHAPTER SIX

INTERPERSONAL BEHAVIORS FOR MINING GROUP GOLD: A SHARED RESPONSIBILITY

CHAPTER OBJECTIVE

➤ To present a set of interpersonal behaviors essential to conducting effective group sessions: Group task behaviors, group maintenance behaviors, and gate-keeping processes.

INTRODUCTION

Geronimo, a fierce warrior and chief of the Apaches who campaigned against the white settlers during the 1880s, was wise and caring toward his tribe. One day a young brave, a handsome, athletic, but self-centered 18-year-old, came to Geronimo and asked what was required to become a man in the warrior's eyes.

A few days later, Geronimo received the young brave at the most sacred spot in the tribal burial grounds. They spoke about the kind of life the boy had lived to that point. Geronimo then served a special tealike drink made from an ancient recipe of herbs and spices. He poured the brave's cup full and kept on pouring. The drink overflowed and soaked into the ground.

After watching a bit, the brave could no longer contain himself. "Geronimo," he exclaimed, "stop pouring. The cup is overfull. No more will go in."

"Like this cup," Geronimo said, "your mind is full of your own judgments, opinions, values, beliefs, and speculations. How can I possibly teach you how to be a man until you empty your cup first?"

This simple tale serves as a fitting introduction to this chapter on interpersonal behaviors. Like the young brave, our heads are full of judgments, opinions, values, beliefs, and speculations about interpersonal behaviors. After all, since the minute we were born, we have been interacting with others. If there is one thing we can claim to be expert in, it is interpersonal behaviors. We have a lifetime of experience in this activity.

Before reading any further do as Geronimo would ask, and "empty your cup a little." Make room for some new perspectives and insights into interpersonal behaviors. Make room so you can look at these interpersonal behaviors through the eyes of a miner of group gold whose intent is to help the group cash in on its collective wisdom.

SETTING THE STAGE

As emphasized in Chapter 3, the manager (acting as primary facilitator), along with every other group member, must share the responsibility for group facilitation. An excellent starting point for shared facilitation is learning and using the interpersonal behaviors and processes for group sessions discussed in this chapter.[1]

By practicing these behaviors, along with the gate-keeping processes to appropriately regulate group participation, all members can help strengthen the group's ability to share and process information.

In order for any group to be productive, it must give attention to task accomplishment. That is, the work of different members must be coordinated and combined so that everyone is pulling together to attain the desired outcomes of the group session. At the same time, the group also must be mindful of the emotional and personal welfare needs of the members. If not, the group jeopardizes its ability to accomplish its task. Most seriously, if proper maintenance behaviors are not performed, the survival of the group is threatened.

Although these task and maintenance behaviors and gate-keeping processes are a shared responsibility, the primary facilitator must be especially tuned in to these behaviors and processes and do his or her best to role model them while facilitating.

While many benefits will accrue to the group that learns, understands, and routinely practices the interpersonal behaviors described in this chapter, four stand out.

Teamwork. Using the behaviors outlined here increases the collaborative capacity of team members. This is a major payoff. Lack of interactive skills among those participating in a group session can carry an enormous price tag; just one person can interfere with the ability of the entire group to achieve its desired outcomes. Collaboration is an essential part of teamwork. Proper use of the interpersonal behaviors and processes fosters collaboration.

A climate of openness and trust. Another key benefit arising from effective interpersonal behavior is the development of an environment in which everyone in the group is encouraged to identify and communicate problems. Messengers bearing bad news are not shot. Rather, they are welcomed so that issues can be resolved as early as possible instead of keeping them covered up until they precipitate a major crisis. A positive climate is built because the gate is opened to help people enter the discussion, personal attacks are few, and differences are mediated by the group. Good listening is directly demonstrated by each person's ability to accurately test comprehension, summarize various points of view, and build on another's idea or proposal.

A fuller understanding of the subject. An additional benefit derived from appropriate use of the interpersonal behaviors and processes is that they help ensure that debate and discussion is objective, orderly, and leads to logical conclusions.

Mistakes due to misunderstandings or incomplete information are minimized.

A greater commitment to the final decision. The fourth payback from properly using the behaviors associated with the task, maintenance, and process actions is commitment. Since employing these behaviors helps to involve everyone in the group's deliberation, there is a greater commitment to the final decision along with a greater chance of a successful implementation.

Before we discuss specific behaviors, look at Exhibit 6–1 to familiarize yourself with the material.

THE GROUP TASK BEHAVIORS

The task component encompasses 10 behaviors, all of which are concerned with a group's efforts to define and accomplish desired outcomes. In order to enhance your understanding of the various task-oriented behaviors, a short definition along with several examples of each behavior is provided.

Exhibit 6–1: INTERPERSONAL BEHAVIORS AND PROCESSES FOR EFFECTIVE GROUP SESSIONS

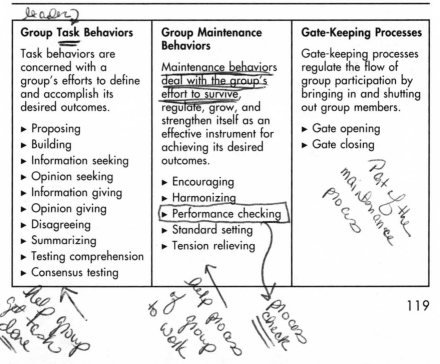

Group Task Behaviors	Group Maintenance Behaviors	Gate-Keeping Processes
Task behaviors are concerned with a group's efforts to define and accomplish its desired outcomes.	Maintenance behaviors deal with the group's effort to survive, regulate, grow, and strengthen itself as an effective instrument for achieving its desired outcomes.	Gate-keeping processes regulate the flow of group participation by bringing in and shutting out group members.
▶ Proposing ▶ Building ▶ Information seeking ▶ Opinion seeking ▶ Information giving ▶ Opinion giving ▶ Disagreeing ▶ Summarizing ▶ Testing comprehension ▶ Consensus testing	▶ Encouraging ▶ Harmonizing ▶ Performance checking ▶ Standard setting ▶ Tension relieving	▶ Gate opening ▶ Gate closing

Proposing. A behavior that initiates a new idea, proposition, or suggestion to spark group action. Proposing is vital at the beginning of a session to get the group moving, and it is also indispensable when the group gets bogged down or when it needs to look at another aspect of the issue.

"I suggest we begin by reviewing last year's figures."

"Here's my idea: let's combine Districts 1 and 2 and place responsibility for both within a new position called Senior District Coordinator."

leads to an intended action

Building. A behavior that takes a group member's proposal, suggestion, or idea and then extends, develops, or expands it to enhance its value. *values*

(Building on the first suggestion above)

"Then we could compare them with this year's figures and have Chad explain the variances."

(Building on the second proposal above)

"Good. That would also allow us to promote Sisler into the Senior District Coordinator slot for a two-year developmental assignment that will prepare her for the Assistant Superintendent position."

Information seeking. A behavior that solicits facts, data, experiences, or clarification from others.

"How many 100 percent attendance days did we have in our middle school last year?"

"Who approved Traynor's expense report?"

Opinion seeking. A behavior that solicits values, beliefs, or sentiments from others.

"David, what are your thoughts on having the building administrators deliver the half-day Disciplinary Procedures Workshop to their own staffs?"

"Noreen, what do you think will happen to the College Relations Program when Cobb leaves?"

Information giving. A behavior that offers facts, data, experiences, or clarification to others.

"Our inspection cost alone on those engines is $43 per unit."

"When I worked at Sajar Plastics, our six janitors were responsible for meeting with vendors, testing their products, and determining which cleaning supplies to purchase."

Opinion giving. A behavior that offers values, beliefs, or sentiments to others.

"I say let's go with it! Brillson is a strict prescription-only drug; those doctors who don't feel it's safe don't have to prescribe it."

"I don't believe the relocation of Teacher Center personnel will increase their morale one iota."

Disagreeing. A behavior that provides direct opposition to, or raises doubts and objections about, an issue (NOT the person who presents it). Technically, disagreeing occurs as a form of information giving or opinion giving; however, since it is such a powerful force—the key to a group's critical thinking—disagreeing is shown here as a distinct task behavior to heighten your awareness of its value.

"I don't buy into Wagner's proposal because it requires a number of my people, who already are putting in six to eight hours of overtime per week, to also work Sundays for the next six months."

"I cannot support having Hornsby observe our team-building session since he is not a member of our immediate group."

Summarizing.   A behavior that reiterates the content of previously shared dialogue in condensed form.

"Then, to review our discussion, we've agreed to order the machine, train the appropriate personnel, and evaluate the results in six weeks."

"So, in a nutshell, we've agreed that there is little advantage to reviewing the Social Studies curriculum this school year unless Foxx Publishing can guarantee delivery of materials by September 1."

Testing comprehension.   A behavior that poses a question in order to establish whether a previous communication has been correctly understood.

"In other words, you're telling me you get nervous when you have to make repeat calls to parents about absenteeism, right?"

"So, are you saying that if I get the revisions to you by 3 tomorrow afternoon, you'll have my report typed by 5 P.M. that same day?"

General agreement

Consensus testing.   A behavior that periodically tests whether the group has reached consensus or whether more discussion of the issue is required.

"Do we now have consensus that we will extend this staff meeting another hour? I'll go right around the table: Christy, . . ."

"Let's see if everyone either can agree with, or can agree to support, the most popular alternative—moving the copier next to the library. I'll start with Tris and go right across the room. Tris? . . ."

GROUP MAINTENANCE BEHAVIORS

The maintenance component incorporates five behaviors associated with the operation of the group *as a group*. These maintenance-oriented behaviors deal with the group's efforts to survive, regulate, grow, and strengthen itself as an effective instrument for achieving desired outcomes. A definition plus several examples of each behavior is given below.

Encouraging. A behavior that supports, agrees with, or recognizes the contributions of others.

> "Carol and Janice, your budget presentation to the School Board was incisive, well-organized, and documented to the hilt. You've both proven you are ready for more difficult assignments."

> "Yes, that's it! You're right, we can do it together. It's risky, but I know we are capable of working out our mission, goals, and operating principles as a team."

Harmonizing. A behavior that attempts to reconcile disagreements or conflict by mediating differences between group members, pointing out the strengths of alternative solutions, or searching for common elements of agreement in opposing positions.

> "I don't see this as an either/or issue. We can have both! We can take 20 percent of the budget surplus, and with matching funds from the state, we can remodel the old fire station and turn it into a centrally located day-care center. Then, we can take the remainder of the surplus and build a larger more up-to-date fire station."

> We are all in agreement that more privacy is necessary for the 10 of you, but permanent walls are inflexible and costly. Eight-foot dividers and soft background music should accomplish the same results. What do you think?"

Performance Checking. A behavior that suspends task operations in order to examine where the group stands in relation to achieving its desired outcomes, to determine how the team members feel about the group's progress in attempting to accomplish its desired outcomes, to air feelings and conflicts, or to evaluate the session at its conclusion.

"I would like to stop our process for a few minutes. Willie, Mickey, Duke, all three of you are certainly upset over the criteria we are generating to select a replacement for Gehringer. Our group really can't move forward unless we understand what your 'pinches' are. If you'll share them with the group, I'll write them on the flip chart so that the three of you will know the rest of us truly understand where you're coming from and why."

"Performance check please! We said we would complete our force field analysis by 3:30; it's now 3:20 and we have at least another 45 minutes worth of work to do. I'm frustrated and feel like quitting at 3:30. I believe we need to discuss where to go from here."

Standard Setting. A behavior that expresses standards for the group and applies these standards to improve the quality of the group process.

"We're getting into groupthink. If we're going to make the best possible decision, we have to increase our critical thinking and take a harder look at what might happen if we go to market now versus six months from now."

"Before Beverly begins, I would like to remind everyone of our groundrule for getting the most out of presentations. We'll allow Beverly to complete her presentation before we discuss content. Only ask questions of clarification during the present portion."

Tension Relieving. A behavior that eases tensions and increases the enjoyment of group members by joking, suggesting breaks, or proposing fun approaches to group work.

"Whew, that was difficult! Let's take a 15-minute break and get our blood circulating again."

"Why don't we hold our next all-day staff meeting at the cabin in Webster Park and then have a picnic when we're finished?"

THE GATE-KEEPING PROCESSES

Unlike the task and maintenance behaviors, the gate-keeping processes do not have content per se. The two processes of gate opening and gate closing can only occur in conjunction with a task or maintenance behavior. In other words, the content for the gate-opening and gate-closing processes is provided by the actual task or maintenance behavior enacted at that point.

When individuals gate close each other's verbal communications, they often do so by verbally interrupting. These interruptions cannot occur in a vacuum. They occur because someone has utilized a task-oriented behavior such as proposing, giving information, giving opinions, disagreeing, and the like. They also can occur because someone has introduced a maintenance-oriented behavior such as encouraging, harmonizing, performance checking, etc. to bring about the gate closing.

The same holds true for gate opening. The only difference is that behaviors such as seeking information, seeking opinions, testing comprehension, consensus testing, performance checking, and tension relieving are used for bringing in others rather than shutting them out.

Gate Opening. This process uses a task or maintenance behavior as a means for directly including another individual in the discussion or for increasing the individual's opportunity to contribute to the discussion.

"Jeanne, have you anything to say on this one?"

"Barry, we haven't heard your thoughts on changing from a 7th- and 8th-grade middle school to one covering grades 7 through 9. What's your position?"

Gate Closing. This process uses a task or maintenance behavior as a means for directly excluding another individual from the discussion or for reducing the individual's opportunity to contribute to the discussion.

John: "How do you feel about our office move, Bob?"

Bob: "Well, from my perspective, I'm hopeful . . ."

125

> **Kathi:** "John, I've told you a hundred times we'll be the forgotten group in that remote location!"

Kathi has gate closed Bob to insert her opinion.

> **Terry:** "Steve, do you have the figures?"
>
> **Steve:** "Yes, we sold 451 units in . . ."
>
> **Jesse:** "And as always you double counted the . . ."
>
> **Terry:** "Please, Jesse, Steve has the floor. Let's give him time to complete his review."

In the first part of this interaction, Jesse dysfunctionally gate-closed Steve. However, in the second part, Terry productively gate closed Jesse to restore Steve as the rightful "owner of the airwaves" so he could finish his review.

A synopsis of all task and maintenance behaviors and both gate-keeping processes are shown in the chapter summary as a learning aid.

TIPS FOR SUCCESSFUL USE

Balance Is Required. In order for a group to define and accomplish its desired outcomes, a balance between the task and maintenance behaviors must be sustained. Additionally, the gate-keeping processes must be employed at times to bring in individuals who are quiet and to shut out, in a productive way, individuals who are interrupting and/or dominating the group session.

There is no right or wrong answer regarding the proper mix among the task, maintenance, and gate-keeping components. All are important. Some group sessions benefit from emphasizing certain behaviors over others. The best balance will vary depending on the different circumstances surrounding the particular agenda item, issue, or problem to be solved.

Stop Task; Invoke Performance Checking. Another noteworthy point regarding use of the task-oriented and maintenance-oriented behaviors is that at any time during a group session—

especially when the task is a difficult, complex one—the group may be forced to do a performance check and confront group maintenance problems. Quite often this entails working through the "feelings" stage of the "feelings, facts, solutions" sequence that is covered in the next chapter.

The central idea, however, is that the effective group stops its task-oriented process, calls attention to specific group process problems, and takes action to reduce or eliminate these stumbling blocks. After this is done, the group can refocus—often with greater unity—on the task behaviors and move forward with the "facts" and "solutions" stages.

The manager and all group members must share the responsibility for recognizing the need, and for taking the initiative, to call for a performance check.

Moderation Is the Key.   Finally, moderation is critical to successfully performing any of the described behaviors and processes. The strength and utility of any of them is impaired if it is used too much or too little, or used to thwart the group from reaching its desired outcomes.

THE MANAGER'S CRUCIAL ROLE

Attaining a reflexive, or unconscious, ability to use these group behaviors takes time and patience, since, in many cases, the manager and the group members will be required to practice behaviors that are new and/or awkward for them. The discussion that follows outlines key steps for instilling excellent interactive skills in a family group.

Role Modeling

Whatever degree of success a group will have in routinely performing behaviors associated with the task, maintenance, and gate-keeping functions will depend to a large extent on the manager (or in the case of committees, task forces, etc., the designated chairperson).

As the person with formal authority, you will be watched by your team members. They will take their behavioral cues from you. Therefore, you need to take the initiative and role model these behaviors to the best of your ability at every appropriate opportunity.

There is a good reason for you to initiate the use of the behaviors via personal action: it legitimizes these behaviors for everyone else on the team. I've used the following story many times in workshops to impress upon managers the single most important factor leading to success in role modeling the interpersonal behaviors and processes.

In the city of Baghdad lived Hakeem, the Wise One. Many people went to him for counsel, which he gave freely to all and asked nothing in return. There came to him a young man who had spent much but received little. The young man said: "Tell me, Oh Wise One, what shall I do to get the most for which I spend?"

Hakeem answered, "A thing that is bought or sold has no value unless it contains that which cannot be bought or sold. Look for the Priceless Ingredient."

"But what is this Priceless Ingredient?" asked the young man.

The Wise One answered him. "My son, the Priceless Ingredient of every transaction in the marketplace is the honor and integrity of the person who sells it. Consider his name before you buy."

How well the behaviors are performed is not as critical as the Priceless Ingredient—the honesty and integrity inherent in their performance. In working with family groups at all organizational levels, my personal experience validates the following principle over and over: group members will invariably respond more positively, and with greater openness, to the family group manager (or any group member, for that matter) who makes unpolished but sincere attempts to practice the interpersonal behaviors, as opposed to the manager who mechanically performs them well, but does so with an aura of hidden agendas, double meanings, and self-serving manipulations.

Encouraging

Besides making a genuine effort to role-model, it is also imperative that the manager use the maintenance behavior of encouraging and stimulate all members to use the interpersonal behaviors and processes with sensitivity and authenticity. Each effort that a group member makes to carry out some of the more troublesome behaviors, like summarizing, disagreeing without getting personal, testing comprehension, standard setting, tension relieving, and productive gate closing, must be recognized immediately with positive feedback.

The recognition does not need to be given with a lot of fanfare. Giving simple, straightforward acknowledgments throughout the group session is all that is required.

"Thank you, Earl, that was a crisp summary of some complex issues."

"That was a difficult topic to reach consensus on, but we were able to disagree without getting personal—that was a big plus."

"Ellen, your testing of comprehension on those two key items short-circuited a major misunderstanding that was developing between us. Nice going."

"You're right, we did agree as a group to spend 10 minutes at the end of each session reviewing our group processes. Thanks for reminding us."

"Good point. We certainly could use a break now."

Unsuccessful attempts by group members to enact the behaviors and processes should not be punished; rather they should be used as a learning experience. This point can be illustrated by the following example.

Assume the group is confused and an individual attempts to summarize the various issues in order to clarify the situation and reduce confusion; however, the person's summary takes an inordinate amount of time, is convoluted, and does nothing to reduce the confusion. At times such as this, you have a tremendous opportunity to "make lemonade out of lemons."

Thank the individual for making an attempt to help reduce confusion, highlight at least one point from the person's comments, then ask if anyone else has other thoughts on the subject being discussed.

> "Dave, thanks for trying to help us determine the main issues concerning our sales strategy. Your point about the impending reorganization is critical. Does anyone else have other thoughts that would help summarize the key issues?"

Coaching

Remember the Priceless Ingredient: the honesty and integrity of the interaction is more important than the skill in doing it. Nevertheless, using the example above, a little private, post-session coaching would be valuable to Dave, to help him do a better job of summarizing next time. The basic process is a very simple and nonthreatening one. At the first appropriate one-on-one opportunity, you should help the individual review what he or she did, what the results were, and what might be done differently next time. Above all, the group member should be urged to try out the behavior again—and again!

As a group matures, or if there are group members who already have refined their abilities to effectively use the task and maintenance behaviors and the gate-keeping processes, the responsibility for practicing these behaviors must be shared. You should not be expected to do it alone!

LIGHTENING THINGS UP

What follows are several classic interactions that I have witnessed over the years, where a variety of the interpersonal behaviors were used quite humorously.

In one lively discussion I was participating in, Mary started to speak but, after saying only two words, was gate closed by

Ken. Actually they both started to speak at the same time and Mary stopped. Ken noticed what had happened and, after pausing for a second or two, recovered beautifully. Looking directly at Mary, he replied in the sincerest tone, "Not to gate close you Mary, but let me build on what you were about to say!" It took five minutes for the laughter to die down.

At a project team meeting, Art, a new member of the team, was extremely vocal. He had opinions about everything. Some of his ideas were good, but many others bordered on babbling. I could see that Bill, the project team leader, was getting irritated. Finally, Bill, in a firm but friendly tone of voice, said, "Art, I'd like to bring you in; you've been silent for two minutes." Art was about to respond, but before he could say anything, Bill continued: "However, we are out of time on this topic." Everyone had a good laugh. Art got the message. Then, at the meeting's conclusion, Bill held a short coaching and counseling session with Art to iron out expectations regarding Art's behavior at future meetings.

This anecdote is a perfect example of the maintenance behavior of tension relieving. I was facilitating a senior-level task force that was trying to decide whether a particular part should be made at the Webster, New York, manufacturing facility or be produced offshore in the Pacific Basin. This was a complex, very serious issue, and the atmosphere was all business. After three hours of presentations and discussions, the task force chairman announced, "Well we finally have defined two specific alternatives. Now, before I do the consensus testing, I'd like to summarize. What you've told me is: alternative one will lead to despair and utter hopelessness, and alternative two will lead to total extinction! Members of the task force, let's pray we have the wisdom to decide correctly."

At that instant, the roof came down. The whole atmosphere lightened up, and even though consensus was not achieved immediately, the group was sparked to a greater effort. At the next session, the task force all agreed on a win/win course of action.

The following interaction is a prime example of seeking and giving information. Rochester, New York, winters are nasty. In mid-February, a manager there received a fax from one of her team members. The fax read, "Stuck in Hawaii for several days due to a tropical storm. What should I do?" The manager sent back a fax reading, "Start vacation as of yesterday."

This final episode was related to me by a manager attending one of my workshops, and it's a terrific example of testing comprehension. The president of a company addressed the employees of the plant. "I know all of you are worried about your jobs now that we have restructured and installed all of our robots. I can understand that you are quite concerned that these robots will eliminate your jobs. Well, I'm happy to say, that won't happen. This company values its human assets. Not only will no one be let go, but you will only have to come to work on Thursdays. Think of it! You will only have to work on Thursday to receive a full week's pay!"

From the back of the room an employee asked, "You mean *every* Thursday?"

For your convenience, all 15 interpersonal behaviors and the two gate-keeping processes are reviewed in the chapter summary. Then, as is the custom in this book, the Notes Worksheet concludes the chapter.

CHAPTER SIX SUMMARY:

GROUP TASK BEHAVIORS

BEHAVIOR	DEFINITION	EXAMPLE
Proposing	Initiating a new idea, proposition, or suggestion to spark group action.	"Let's start by introducing ourselves."
Building	Taking a group member's proposal, suggestion, or idea, and then extending, developing, or expanding it to enhance its value.	(Building on the proposal above) "And then tell one wild or crazy thing we've done in the last 12 months."
Information seeking	Soliciting facts, data, experiences, or clarification from others.	"What would it cost to ship this package over night?"
Information giving	Offering facts, data, experiences, or clarification to others.	"$16.75 and it will be there by noon tomorrow."
Opinion seeking	Soliciting values, beliefs, or sentiments from others.	"What do you think about Shurgot's chances of winning the election?"
Opinion giving	Offering values, beliefs, or sentiments to others.	"Unless Shurgot takes a more liberal view on tax reform, I don't think he has any chance of winning."
Disagreeing	Providing direct opposition to, or raising doubts about, an issue not the person.	"No way, we'll have to find an area other than travel to cut expenses."
Summarizing	Reiterating the content of previously shared dialogue in condensed form.	"So, what we'll do then is: take legal action; take it before May; and, issue a writ in the chairman's name."
Testing comprehension	Posing a question in order to establish whether a previous communication has been correctly understood.	"Are you saying that I can use the yearly dividends from my policy to increase the death benefit on Marianne's policy?"
Consensus testing	Periodically testing whether the group has reached consensus or whether more discussion of the issue is required.	"Alternative six seems to be everyone's favorite, let's see if we have consensus. Ed . . ."

GROUP MAINTENANCE BEHAVIORS

BEHAVIOR	DEFINITION	EXAMPLE
Encouraging	Supporting, agreeing with, or recognizing the contributions of others.	"Excellent point Wayland, I wish I had thought of it."
Harmonizing	Reconciling disagreements and conflict by mediating differences between group members, pointing out the strengths of alternative solutions, or searching for common elements of agreement in opposing positions.	"Ed's proposal costs us $50,000 but could be completed within four weeks. Don's idea costs us $45,000 but would take six weeks to complete. Both are within budget and schedule constraints." The key tradeoffs are . . ."
Performance checking	Suspending task operations to tend to internal group processes.	"We're definitely confused. Let's stop for a moment and reaffirm what this decision *is* and *is not* about."
Standard setting	Expressing standards for the group and applying these standards to improve the quality of the group's process.	"From now on, all staff meetings begin at 8:00 A.M. sharp."
Tension relieving	Easing tensions and increasing the enjoyment of group members by joking, suggesting breaks, or proposing fun approaches to work!	"This meeting has gone on long enough in this conference room. Let's finish it over margaritas at the Red Onion."

GATE-KEEPING PROCESSES

PROCESS	DEFINITION	EXAMPLE
Gate opening	Utilizing a task or maintenance behavior to include another person in the discussion.	"Ashley, you've been quiet, in what other areas might we cut costs?"
Gate closing	Utilizing a task or maintenance behavior to exclude another person from the discussion.	(Sandi) You turn left at the first light . . . (Luke) Naw, go to the third light, hang a left and then . . . Luke has gate-closed Sandi.

Tips for Successful Use

- Balance is required
- Stop task; invoke performance checking
- Moderation is the key

The Manager's Crucial Role

- Role modeling
- Encouraging
- Coaching

Notes Worksheet: DEVELOP WRITTEN RESPONSES TO THE TWO
ITEMS LISTED BELOW

What do you feel are the main learning points from Chapter 6?	Elaborate on why you feel these points are key.

Note

1. The interpersonal behaviors and processes model presented in this chapter draws from the following research.

   K. D. Benne and P. Sheats, "Functional Roles of Group Members," *Journal of Social Issues* 4(2) (1948): pp. 42–47.

   R. Likert, *New Patterns of Management* (New York: McGraw-Hill, 1965), pp. 162–77.

   J. K. Brilhart, *Effective Group Discussion* (Dubuque, IA: William C. Brown Publishers, 1967).

   A. G. Athos and R. E. Coffey, *Behavior in Organizations: A Multidimensional View* (Englewood Cliffs, NJ: Prentice-Hall, 1968), pp. 115–27.

   N. Rackham, P. Honey, and C. Colbert, *Developing Interactive Skills* (Guidsborough, Northampton, England: Wellers Publishing, 1971).

   D. W. Johnson and F. P. Johnson, *Joining Together: Group Therapy and Group Skills* (Englewood Cliffs, NJ: Prentice-Hall, 1975); pp. 18–30, 40–42.

   L. P. Bradford, *Making Meetings Work* (La Jolla, CA: University Associates, 1976), pp. 35–46.

   P. S. Goodman and E. J. Conlon, "Observation of Meetings," in S. E. Seashore, et al., eds., *Assessing Organizational Change: A Guide to Methods, Measures, and Practices* (New York: John Wiley & Sons, 1983), pp. 353–67.

   W. G. Dyer, *Strategies for Managing Change* (Reading, MA: Addison-Wesley, 1984), pp. 127–33.

   "Building a Team Through Effective Meetings," *Trainer's Workshop: A Publication of the American Management Association* 1(5) (November 1986): pp. 22–33.

   E. H. Schein, *Process Consultation: Its Role in Organizational Development*, Vol. 1 (Reading, MA: Addison-Wesley, 1988), pp. 49–56.

CHAPTER SEVEN

K EEPING THE GOLD MINE PRODUCTIVE IN THE FACE OF EMOTION: FEELINGS, FACTS, SOLUTIONS

CHAPTER OBJECTIVES

➤ To describe the components of the "feelings, facts, solutions" productivity sequence.

➤ To underscore the critical role that feelings play during a group session.

➤ To emphasize the need to deal with feelings when they arise.

➤ To present a set of basic how-to tips and techniques for facilitating the feelings portion of the "feelings, facts, solutions" sequence.

INTRODUCTION

Few things in a facilitator's tool kit are more important than an understanding of this simple sequence of group behavior: *feelings, facts, solutions.* This sequence originally was set forth by Strauss and Sayles[1] to describe the three major stages of the nondirective interview. This sequence also can be applied to groups; it provides the road map for successful facilitation, and its value as a conceptual tool cannot be overstated.

UNDERSTANDING THE COMPONENTS

Feelings

When a group is in the "feelings" or "emotions" phase, it is pointless to say, "Let's keep feelings out of this" because the group is already expressing them. To handle this stage properly, feelings must be accepted, acknowledged as real, and processed in an organized manner.

Should you attempt to press on with the agenda or move forward with problem identification and analysis without first adequately processing group members' feelings, your efforts will be resisted. The group will continue to focus on war stories, anecdotes, monologues, debates, and discussions that release feelings without regard for the purpose, desired outcomes, and agenda of the session.

With feelings getting in the way, the group's ability to move along to the more rational and disciplined process of presenting and analyzing the facts, developing potential solutions to problems, and making decisions about which of those to implement is severely restricted.

Any time a group goes into the "feelings" phase, you need to encourage individuals to express their emotions, process them in an organized way, and move into phase two—facts. If this is not done, the session may get bogged down in a directionless emotional confrontation.

Facts

Having had a chance to ventilate feelings in a structured way, the group is now ready to develop and analyze the facts in a less emotional, more objective manner. You are in a position to help the group generate and use facts, and to identify and then analyze the problem.

138

As Sayles and Strauss point out, "Facts may be hard to obtain but at least they are subject to objective inquiry, and it is usually easier to get agreement on facts than it is to get agreement on opinions. Actually, one may lead to the other."[2]

Bales reinforces the importance of facts by stating, "A rich background of common facts lays the groundwork for the development of common inferences and sentiments, and out of these, common decisions can grow. No decision rests on 'facts' alone, but there is no better starting point."[3]

In any situation, be it discussion, problem solving, or decision making, facts can be handled more smoothly and effectively once feelings have been addressed. Moreover, the group is less likely to fall back into the "feelings" phase and thus require further catharsis.

Solutions

Once the facts have been assembled and the problem has been identified and analyzed, the final stage is reached. The group is ready to generate potential solutions, select one of them, and make decisions about implementing it. In facilitating through this phase, you can take advantage of the tools and techniques presented here as well as those in Chapters 5, 6, and 8.

Movement Between Phases

Feelings—facts—solutions is the three-phase sequence to group productivity. The group may, of course, switch back and forth between phases as different agenda items, problems, or issues are considered, or as new aspects of the same issue are considered.

Most importantly, don't waste time trying to isolate the facts before the group has had a chance to express feelings and go through catharsis. Feelings color facts, and as long as the group is emotionally excited, its ability to approach the subject rationally is diminished.

Similarly, you need to avoid the common tendency to facilitate jumping to a solution before getting all the facts.

Remember too that the group will not always have strong feelings on every agenda item. In those instances, a quick movement into the "facts" phase is appropriate.

Finally, there may be times when the outcome for a particular agenda item is merely to discuss the topic as thoroughly as possible; a solution is not required. In those cases, you will only have to help the group complete the "feelings" and "facts" phases. In most situations, however, the manager facilitates the group through the traditional sequence: feelings, facts, solutions.

Know Thyself

Before moving ahead to present the specific processes for facilitating group feelings, a word about the family group manager, as a person, is in order. In order to be an effective facilitator of the group's feelings, you must comprehend your own biases as well as the triggers for them. In other words, being able to help a group work through its feelings so that it can progress to the "facts" and "solutions" phases begins with "knowing thyself." The manager or chairperson facilitating the session is human and, as such, is subject to the same human frailties as the other group members. However, by understanding your own defense mechanisms and biases, you can make an effort to control them and steer clear of the numerous opportunities to get sucked into the emotional fray as a full-blown "feelings" participant. When this happens, facilitation invariably is nil.

Getting trapped in the emotion of the situation is, for the most part, unintentional. Still, whether unintentional or not, the results are the same. The manager and the group participants wind up engaged in a heated, and often prolonged, discussion without anyone paying attention to facilitation. Your primary defense against being unwittingly drawn into the thick of the emotional exchange is to "know thyself."

Schein, speaking about himself as a consultant, makes some poignant comments on the topic of self-awareness. "As a consultant I have to observe myself in action over a period of time and get corrective feedback from others in order to identify the systematic biases in how I perceived things. Once I know what those biases are I can take greater care in checking things out before reacting to them."[4]

Regarding the need to identify one's own emotional response biases, Schein artfully makes his point.

> If I have a systematic bias to respond to certain kinds of data with certain kinds of emotions, I need to know what that bias is in order to judge its appropriateness to any given situation. For example, if I tend to respond defensively and get angry whenever a client challenges me or tells me I am wrong, I need to recognize this as a bias and learn to control or compensate for that feeling if my judgement tells me that it would not be helpful to the consultation [or facilitation] process to get into an argument with the client. . . . In order to make choices and decide what will be most facilitative in a given situation, one needs to know one's biases.[5]

Schein does not imply that learning about, accepting, and controlling one's biases is an easy thing to do. It isn't. However, it is crucial for every family group manager or group leader to make an honest, ongoing effort to do so in order to elevate his or her ability to facilitate the "feelings, facts, solutions" sequence to group productivity.

UNDERSTANDING VENTING STYLES

Besides knowing your personal biases, you need to be aware of typical venting styles. People do bring forth their catharsises differently. Over the years I've built a mental map that has helped me recognize and accept the broad divergence in venting styles. In no way is this a scientific profile based on controlled psychological or personality research. It is just a simple tool I've evolved that has proven useful on more than one occasion when feelings flared and I needed a way to quickly focus on what was happening. Tying back to the previous "know thyself" theme, this little model will help you better understand your own venting tendencies. Knowing this, you can be more tolerant, accepting, and encouraging of those whose styles are different from your own.

Exhibit 7–1 shows a four cell matrix that breaks venting into four styles. When in a feelings state, a person or group vents, to varying degrees, on two different levels—the "words expressed" level (open or guarded) and the "emotions expressed" level (open or guarded). The words and emotions dimensions, when taken in all combinations, lead to four primary styles.

Expressers (Open words; Open emotions).   As their name implies, expressers freely vent when in a feelings state. Their words and emotions are both congruent and open. You will get good insight as to where they stand (words) and why they believe so strongly in their convictions (emotions). I've found that because they have no problem opening up and getting it out, their venting is usually short lived. They just want to get things off their chests, and then they are ready to move ahead. With expressers, pay attention to the words behind their emotions, many good ideas for problem solving and decision making are often brought forward.

Directors (Open words; Guarded emotions).   Directors don't really vent with a lot of emotion; outwardly they appear relatively calm. Instead, they vent using strong, powerful words

Exhibit 7–1: FOUR VENTING STYLES

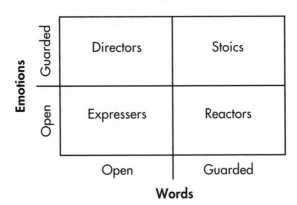

like "exploit," "combat ready," "take charge," "arrogance," "challenge," "eradicate," etc. They speak quickly, confidently, and forcefully. They are good at using body language to emphasize their words; for example, ticking off each point by reciting "point a," "point b," "point c," while simultaneously flicking out their fingers or tapping their pen on the table for each point. Directors have no patience for incompetence, time wasting, confusion, or bureaucracy. They readily vent over these topics. Also, they tend to vent early.

Reactors (Guarded words; Open emotions). They can blow off steam at any time if something doesn't set well with them. Their emotions will be clear. Body language, facial expressions, tone of voice will all reinforce the emotion being displayed. However, as opposed to expressers, the words of reactors will often be indirect and obscure. While their feelings are clearly expressed, the reasons or meaning behind them are far more difficult to clarify. It is often a facilitation challenge not to become frustrated with reactors; but, if they get any sense that others are not concerned with their emotion, they may express even stronger feelings.

Stoics (Guarded words; Guarded emotions). Stoics may have strong feelings, but they are unlikely to let you know about them early. Outwardly they appear calm, and they aren't saying anything that indicates strong feelings. Inwardly, however, stoics may be churning with emotion, "brewing an emotional outburst" that can catch you by surprise with its suddenness and intensity. Stoics are the opposite of expressers. Be sensitive to body language and tone of voice when they do speak. Their fidgeting, facial expressions, posture, aura of preoccupation, agitated tone of voice and the like, are your best clues that all is not well regarding inner feelings. If you sense something is amiss, it is wise to test your impression by saying something like: "Claudia, I sense you are bothered by the direction this discussion is going;, you seem very uneasy. What's bothering you?" While Claudia may decline the invitation to respond, chances are she probably will begin to open up. It's better to short-circuit the stoic's internal churn as soon as you sense it, rather than letting it fester and explode.

143

PROCESSING FEELINGS EFFECTIVELY

For you, acting as primary facilitator, being able to deal properly with feelings is the single most critical facilitation skill to be honed. As will be shown, the actual techniques and process for handling feelings, regardless of the venting style, are not difficult to carry out. They tend to seem more formidable than they really are because the atmosphere of the "feelings" phase is potentially explosive. Knowing in advance what to do will significantly reduce your sense of intimidation during the emotional portion of a group session.

Getting specific, let us assume that you have just finished outlining the dimensions and history of a complex, controversial subject with which your group must concern itself. At this point, you are at a facilitation crossroads. Depending on the specifics woven into the subject just presented, the group will either move into the "feelings" phase or bypass feelings, at least for now, and get down to the business of working the facts. Through careful planning of the group session's structure and process as described in Chapter 4 and 5, you will have a good understanding of the group and will be able to assess whether the group will need to pass through the "feelings" phase before being able to process the facts objectively. Anticipating that strong feelings are likely to be manifested on this subject—especially among those members who have considerable personal investment—you can set aside some portion of the session to encourage venting and catharsis and then process the feelings along the lines to be recommended in this chapter.

But what happens if, after the subject is presented, strong feelings unexpectedly surface? In other words, feelings weren't planned for. Don't panic; don't discount the feelings and attempt to "bulldoze ahead" with the planned agenda; and, above all, follow the guiding principles presented here.

Arlyn Melcher, chairman of the department of management at Southern Illinois University in Carbondale, has some sound advice regarding the facilitation of feelings.

> A group discussion is not going to be productive as long as strong feelings persist. The way to alleviate this situation is to recognize what is taking place and deal with

it by providing group members with acceptable outlets for venting their emotions. Ask people what they feel and why. Get them to talk; to express their feelings. Above all, remember that logic won't solve an emotional situation. Logic loses to emotion. No matter how long the meeting, a group member cannot be convinced with logic if that person's mind is blocked with emotion. Also, keep in mind that logic is in the "ears of the beholder." What is so logical and intuitively obvious to one individual may not be logical at all to an emotional listener.[6]

The importance of catharsis is underscored by Fisher and Ury.

People obtain psychological release through the simple process of recounting their grievances. If you come home wanting to tell your husband about everything that went wrong at the office, you will become even more frustrated if he says, "Don't bother telling me; I'm sure you had a hard day. Let's skip it." The same is true of group. Letting off steam may make it easier to talk rationally later.[7]

There are four guiding principles that leaders can use to help group members express, and then process, their feelings in a constructive manner regardless of the venting style being used.

Stay Neutral

First and foremost, the family group manager must never get personally involved while in the role of facilitator; however, using the process of hat switching, the manager can provide personal inputs to the content of the discussion. If there is ever a time to keep the role of family group manager separate from that of primary facilitator, a "feelings" discussion is the time. Therefore, whenever feelings do burst forth, the hat that you immediately should reach for is the one labeled *facilitator*. This should almost be reflexive. Feelings in the group trigger the facilitator role in the family group manager. A family group manager drawn into the heat of battle will find it next to impossible to be a neutral processor of "feeling" information at the very time performance of this activity is needed most. But how can the manager as facilitator behave in a neutral manner?

Respect People's Right to Have Their Feelings.   The group members have as much right to their feelings as you have to yours. Keeping this in mind, you must accept the feelings expressed by group members as being legitimate and convey an attitude that both the group members as individuals, and their ideas, are worthy of attention.

You are not required to agree with others' feelings, but simply to accept that they exist. At appropriate points, you can communicate your own thoughts and feelings in response to what has been said. Practicing the art of excellent facilitation, you must demonstrate that the feelings being shared by others deserve to be heard.

Effective techniques to convey both acceptance and personal neutrality include letting the person have his or her say (instead of gate closing), thanking the person for comments made, and practicing the task-oriented behaviors of testing comprehension (to ensure proper understanding) and summarizing (to capture nonjudgmentally what was said).

Encourage and Acknowledge Expression of Feelings.   When group members are in the "feelings" phase, their expressed fears, doubts, anger, inadequacy, frustrations, and viewpoints are exceedingly valuable communications. Therefore, feelings need to be heard and understood. While the thought of encouraging people to express their feelings may be intimidating to many of you, remember that neutrality makes this process easier.

Performing the maintenance behavior of encouraging expression while maintaining neutrality takes discipline but is not difficult. The feelings need to be brought out so they can be understood and processed. The technique for doing this is to acknowledge what is being presented with positive head nods, and simple verbal feedback such as: "I understand," "I see," "true," "that certainly could be," or other similar statements.

Neutrality through the practice of these basic communications pays significant facilitation dividends. By remaining neutral, you maintain the role of primary facilitator, stay detached from any inflammatory content, stimulate the speaker to open up, and leave little or no residue of unexpressed feelings to fester.

Understand Rather Than Evaluate Feelings

For most people—regardless of their organizational role—this is a difficult principle to apply. It is especially troublesome for the family group manager practicing the art of facilitation.

Efficient family group managers are supposed to absorb a mass of information, quickly sort through it, evaluate what has been said or written, pass judgment, and announce a decision. These characteristics have put them on the "fast track" to promotions. Certainly, skillful use of these behaviors is deemed by many to be the mark of a tough, no-nonsense manager.

On the surface at least, the role of the manager as tough decision maker seems to conflict with the role of manager as facilitator, where a premium is placed on listening and understanding. Not only are these roles not in conflict, effectiveness in executing the facilitator role actually strengthens the individual's ability to carry out the family group manager role. Skilled facilitation in getting feelings out, understood, and processed provides a much stronger foundation for making a quality decision than does running roughshod over group members' feelings, misunderstanding their intent, and making value judgments about them on the way to another "tough call." Problems involving communication failures and misunderstandings are less likely to occur if the initial tendencies to evaluate and judge are suspended. No matter which of the four venting styles is used, any person expressing emotion is calling out for the same thing: "Hear me!" "Understand me!" What can a manager specifically do to increase his or her ability to understand feelings rather than evaluate them?

Probe with the Nonevaluative Task-Oriented Interpersonal Behaviors. The task behaviors of seeking information, seeking opinions, building, testing comprehension, and summarizing are excellent techniques for increasing understanding while staying out of an evaluation mode. When a group member

147

expresses a thought with obvious emotional overtones, try to gain a fuller understanding of the statement's content and underlying causes by seeking more information and further clarification.

In addition, you can test for comprehension by nonjudgmentally reflecting the words and the feelings of the message back to its originator to make sure it has been truly understood. "Robyn, what I'm hearing from you is a great deal of frustration with our consensus process because it seems like we're getting nowhere. Am I right in my understanding?"

Finally, using the summarizing technique to recap the group position after a 10- to 15-minute exchange of thoughts and feelings is critical to keep confusion and misunderstandings in check.

Be Sensitive to Verbal and Nonverbal Cues. Quite often during a feelings discussion, you will fail to grasp the verbal and/or nonverbal reactions of group members to the statements being made. Being a miner of group gold requires that you have a sharp "third ear." Recognizing and listening for subtle and indirect reactions—especially with directors and stoics—is essential to gaining a full understanding of what is being said. If these emotional reactions—a sharp tone of voice, a raising and lowering of the speaker's eyebrows, or a tapping of a pen on the table to emphasize certain words—go unheeded, the emotional climate is being inefficiently managed.

As long as the feelings behind the words are ignored by the manager, the group members will keep pulling the group back to the "feelings" phase and never allow the session to move fully into the "facts" phase. Or, if this does not occur, another equally negative response is for those with ignored feelings to withdraw from all discussions and become uninterested, passive members for the remainder of the session. The result is valuable meeting talent is lost.

On the other hand, the manager who recognizes and encourages the expression of feelings not only acknowledges the seriousness of the problem, but also helps make the session's dialogue less reactive and more proactive. Freed from the burden of unexpressed or ignored emotions, the group members become more willing to work on the problem from a "facts" and "solutions" standpoint.

Process Feelings Using Silence, Then Flip Charts

Silence.   When feelings arise and reach the point where formal processing is required, the processing always begins with silence. Before you move ahead to facilitate the group's feelings, a short period of silence is essential. This period of silence allows people to calm down, to reflect on their feelings, and to think before blurting out something that might be regretted later. The need for this period of transition between the arousal of feelings and processing them is elaborated on by Avery, Auvine, Streibel, and Weiss.

> A session spent working with anger, frustration, fear or other unpleasant feelings can start with a few minutes of silence. Each person can use this time to identify and clarify his or her own feelings, and to become composed enough to prevent a destructive interchange later on. Silence is an opportunity for members to think for a moment without distraction, but it has benefits that go beyond the rational thought that occurs during this period. Silence is often soothing, allows members to become "centered," and breaks the flow of a competitive, overexcited interchange. Often during silence, a member will realize that a point he or she was arguing for so urgently is not really that important after all.[8]

With the silence period completed, the processing phase begins. To make it clear that feelings are not being ignored, and to capture what may be invaluable data for use later, you should employ the aid of an indispensable tool—the flip chart. Here are three simple, nonthreatening approaches for processing feelings.

Bring in the whole group.   This method is useful if there is a contingent that is into feelings. You should obtain a statement of the contingent's position and feelings by using the interpersonal behaviors of seeking opinions and information, testing comprehension, and summarizing. Have the scribe write the results on a flip chart. Next, ask the entire group what it thinks about the expressed position and feelings, and have this response written on a flip chart.

Taking all of the data provided by both the contingent and the rest of the group, you then write a summary statement for each side that acknowledges their general position, thank the group members for their participation, and post the summaries. Where appropriate, this information can be used in the later stages of the session.

Round-robin. This approach is good to use when the whole group seems to be in a "feelings" mode, and it's difficult to get a reading as to the general themes of these feelings. As facilitator, go around the room and have group members summarize their feelings on the issue and why they feel that way. Then engage the whole group in categorizing the feelings into common themes. Once this is done, thank the group for its participation and post the information for all to see (as well as for possible use later in the session).

Buzz groups. This technique is expedient when the whole group seems to be into feelings, but it could be threatening to some individuals to expose their feelings on a round-robin basis. To use this approach, break the whole group into buzz groups and let the buzz group members express their feelings to each other. Each buzz group is charged with taking notes on the common themes and choosing a spokesperson to provide a summary of these themes to the whole group. Write down these summary comments, thank the group members for their participation, and post the information for possible future use in the session.

All three methods are analogous to the stream valve on a pressure cooker. They provide a structured means for you to encourage the necessary expression of group feelings without losing control of the session.

More often than not, the feelings that come forth are doubts, concerns, or fears about an action or plan. These feelings arise because one or more of the group members are, in some way, affected by the action or plan. Therefore, if you believe that immediate processing of the posted information is required, work with the group to:

➤ Combine, condense, and refine the concerns list so that all items are discrete.

> Use distributive voting to shorten the list to the three biggest concerns of the group. The mechanics of distributive voting are simple. Participants are given six votes each and are told to distribute them in the following manner: three votes on their number one concern, two votes on their number two concern, and one vote on their number three concern. There is to be no deviation from these voting ground rules. When voting is finished, add up the total number of votes for each item. Circle the three items receiving the highest vote totals to isolate them as the three biggest concerns.

> Hold a positive discussion: one in which the group, working collaboratively, focuses its energies on reducing, eliminating, or avoiding its three biggest concerns.

Many times this information-processing exercise is not necessary. Merely giving group members the opportunity to voice their feelings, to clarify them, to know they are understood, and to discover how others feel is enough to satisfy the participants. Remember, the task of the manager as facilitator is to process the group's feelings—not debate, deny, defend, attack, object to, or question them. When wearing the family group manager's hat, the manager's personal views can be shared.

Refocus the Discussion on the Original Topic and Its Desired Outcomes

After feelings have been vented in a structured way, it's time to refocus. The major tool here is the interpersonal behavior of summarizing. Summarize the main points of the feelings discussion. If the flip chart was used, these sheets can be reviewed. Then recount the outcomes of the original topic. For example, you can refocus the discussion by saying something like, "That was a stimulating discussion on going outside the company to get the video made. It's clear that everyone now feels we should get the job done inside and all but two people feel we should use our own employees to play the parts instead of hiring professional actors. Let's keep these feelings in mind as we continue to look at specific things our department can do to help improve return on assets (ROA) this year."

Sometimes you may have to be assertive in getting the group to refocus on the original topic because of a phenomenon known as the "feelings merry-go-round." Nothing robs a group's energy more than members who constantly repeat their feelings after these feelings have been heard, understood, accepted, written down on a flip chart, and posted.

Bringing a "feelings merry-go-round" to a halt requires that the facilitator reminds the person that he or she has said something several times, shows them that it has been recorded in their own words, asks if there is any new information to add, and if not, moves forward by refocusing on the original topic and its desired outcomes. Pointing to the words on the flip chart page, you could say, "Roy, I know your point is important to you. You've already said that three times, and I've got it written down just the way you wanted it recorded. I accept your feelings. Is there anything new you'd like to add? If not, we must move on and explore other things our group can do to improve ROA this year."

Cutting off a "feelings merry-go-round" is an essential facilitation activity that you will have to carry out from time to time. It requires that you be assertive in taking charge of the situation and stop it before it multiplies into a beast that consumes the whole meeting.

But What If the Family Group Manager Has Strong Thoughts or Feelings on the Subject?

Acting as primary facilitator does not, in any way, isolate the manager from participating in the content aspects of the topic being debated. During the processing of the group's feelings, you may find it essential to share your thoughts or feelings on the issue being discussed. You have every right to add input. However—and this is of utmost importance—*the manager must verbally indicate that he or she is momentarily stepping out of the facilitator role and into the role of formal manager of the group.* This verbal hat switching is necessary in order to avoid any confusion about the source of the message: It is from the manager operating in the role of group manager. For example, while pointing to a flip chart listing the feelings of others, you could, with a great deal of emotion, say:

> After listening to the views of Daneale, Scott, Sean, and Pat, and understanding why they feel the way they do, let me switch hats from facilitator to family group manager and respond this way. I am extremely upset at the very thought of using consultants. It is a waste of $13,000 to use outsiders to teach our *Power of Recognition Workshop.* Consultants have no conception of how our business operates; most of them probably haven't worked one day as a manager in a high-tech company. I can't stand the thought of paying an outsider to do a job we can do better ourselves. I firmly believe we will get acceptable delivery of content, and heck of a lot deeper discussion about practical applications, if we train a group of our own managers to teach the workshop. That's the approach we used at Technicom when I worked there, and it was terrific!

There can be further dialogue between the manager and the other group members. However, the manager cannot lose sight of his or her substantial obligation to the group—to return to the role of primary facilitator and be attentive to the group process. At no time after shifting to the role of manager should you get so heavily drawn into the discussion that your facilitation role is forgotten. Therefore, after an appropriate amount of dialogue, you need to signify a return to the role of primary facilitator and concentrate on assisting the group process as opposed to directly contributing to the content.

In situations where you find yourself personally becoming embroiled in an emotional discussion, but where the group contains an individual who is skilled enough to handle the primary facilitation role and who is not caught up in the heat of the moment, you have the luxury of being able to switch to your manager's role and to assign the primary facilitator's role to this other person. This affords you the opportunity to become fully immersed in the content and emotion of the subject without having to worry about primary facilitation responsibilities. However, after the emotional issue, say staff reductions, is concluded, you should reclaim the role of primary facilitator.

If you are fortunate enough to have facilitation flexibility, it should be taken advantage of when necessary. Still, in the innumerable instances where the role of the primary facilitator cannot be temporarily assigned to another person during a particular discussion, the most effective way for you to facilitate a "feelings" discussion is the one recommended in this chapter. That is, practice a process of controlled entry and exit into and out of the "feelings" discussion while never losing sight of the critical role of primary facilitator.

"Feelings, facts, solutions" is a sequence that does lead to group productivity. When a group hits the "feelings" stage, it is pointless for you to urge movement into the "facts" and "solutions" stages before helping the group deal with its feelings. By providing a practical means for letting the group members vent their feelings and by recording them on a flip chart, you can prevent the session from breaking down into a directionless emotional confrontation.

For most managers, dealing with group feelings is an unpleasant, tension-ridden, and often intimidating chore. Many times the cardinal mistake is made: ignoring the feelings and "getting on with resolving the blasted issues." Managers do this to avoid dealing with emotional issues, as well as in a misguided attempt to keep the meeting on track. However, by facing the situation and following the techniques presented in this chapter, you can significantly increase your chances of successfully handling group feelings.

CARAVAN FREIGHT, INC.: A CASE STUDY

Lloyd Price is business operations manager for Caravan Freight, Inc., a national trucking company with profits of $34 million on revenues of $850 million. Caravan, like so many firms in the highly competitive trucking industry, is faced with unrelenting pressures to keep costs down.

In early January, J. P. Richardson, president of Caravan, sent a memo to his direct reports urging them to "do everything possible—short of downsizing—to trim costs and increase productivity." The goal given to the senior staff was an 11 percent productivity increase, company wide, by year end.

In response to the memo, Lloyd Price decided to set up a strategic planning meeting with his six managers to determine how to deal with Richardson's difficult request. So Lloyd sent out an e-mail memo to his team announcing Richardson's productivity initiative and the key particulars for the four hour strategic planning meeting. He also included information on the session's purpose, desired outcomes, role assignments, and agenda. The meeting was scheduled for the day after tomorrow.

Price's e-mail elicited an angry reply from his billing manager, Cathy Carr (a reactor). The gist of her message was: "You've got to be kidding. If J. P. would just come down from his ivory tower and see the way my team is configured, he'd find out we can't even begin to think about his ridiculous task. It's always take and no give! How can you be productive when you're just a payroll number?" Several other reactors shot other angry e-mails to all team members—including Lloyd. The lid had blown off.

Driving home that night Lloyd admitted to himself that he was feeling frustrated and stressed. While productivity certainly had to be increased, when would the stream of crisis projects end? Caravan also was in the midst of a major restructuring, its quality improvement teams were dying on the vine because management was spread so thin it couldn't provide proper support, and Caravan's parent company had kept all budgets and headcount numbers flat while increasing sales revenue targets by 8 percent for the year.

On the morning of the session, right after Lloyd welcomed the team—but before he could review the purpose, desired outcomes, and agenda—Peter Best, the repair shop manager (a director), spoke up first. Forcefully, point by point, and pounding the table with his fist for each one, he articulated six reasons why he had neither the time, resources, nor desire to commit to this task. Only asking a few simple clarifying questions, Lloyd wrote all of Peter's points on a flip chart.

Ruth Brown (an expressive) chimed in attacking the 11 percent productivity goal as stupid and unrealistic. She cited several productivity studies in the trucking industry that hailed 4 to 6 percent year-over-year productivity gains as being outstanding. She also reminded everyone about November's thoroughly abysmal attitude survey results. Handing out a copy to everyone, she highlighted the "employee motivation and commitment section" where the rating was only 55 percent positive. Then, standing up and waving her arms, she said: "Anger is not a strong enough word to describe how I feel. Totally pissed is better, but it still falls short!" With only positive head nods and reinforcing comments like "good point," "OK," "I've got it noted," etc., Lloyd duly noted all of Ruth's thoughts and feelings on the flip chart.

Jim Lowe (a reactor) said he was going to paint his office door green as a visible protest against Richardson's greed for his big bonus at the expense of the "little guys." Richie Valenzuela (a reactor) told everyone: "I've had it. I'm giving my two week notice right now." Cathy Carr (a reactor) said: "This company has to have a monopoly on stupidity. I just know it does. No company in the world could possibly make dumber decisions, faster, than Caravan!"

Although he felt like he was being indirectly attacked, he wrote their comments on the flip chart, checking back to be sure he was writing down exactly what they were feeling, and tearing the sheets off the pad and taping them to the wall. Then, Lloyd said, "Look, I know how upset you are, I feel the same way. We need to continue to process our feelings, but in a little more structured way. Let's all take a moment of silence, reflect on our feelings, and write them down. After that, I'll go around the room, round-robin style, and capture everyone's feelings by adding them to our chart. If you already have something on the chart from before and want to add to it, that's fine. I'll be fully participating in this exercise myself."

The team did as instructed. When finished, Lloyd called upon Clarence Henry who had been silent throughout the previous discussion. "Clarence, it looked to me like you were getting quite irritated during our team's little outburst a few minutes ago, but you weren't saying anything. I'd really like to hear how you feel about our productivity task." Clarence replied: "Yes, I was upset. Still am. What really fries me is that neither Richardson, you, nor anyone else on the senior staff really appreciates the hoops we have to jump through to accomplish a major request. We get no budget or headcount relief to help us and nothing comes off the plate in terms of current tasks. When will Richardson realize that you can't put ten pounds of garbage in a five pound bag? Furthermore, . . ." (The stoic was getting it out sooner rather than later.)

Lloyd went completely around the room getting everything written down from everyone. At one point, he shared and wrote down his own thoughts from his drive home the other night. He added that he was angry because Richardson had made the productivity decision unilaterally. There had been no discussion. It caught the entire senior staff by surprise.

Throughout the structured venting process, Lloyd, as primary facilitator, and several others from time to time, as secondary facilitators, made sure everyone's feelings were heard, understood, acknowledged as real, and accepted.

When the process was finished, the team had 38 items on three full sheets of paper. The atmosphere in the room had lightened considerably. While people weren't overjoyed, they all admitted they felt better for the opportunity to say what they felt and get it off their chests.

Clarence asked Lloyd what he intended to do with his sheets. Lloyd replied: "I personally don't plan to do anything with them. This is our data. We need to process this information further. Even though it came out as feelings, there is a wealth of ideas on those sheets. I'd like to propose that Clarence, Cathy, Ruth, and Peter take these sheets and consolidate them. Categorize the feelings into buckets according to issues like: aspects of the assignment itself; workload and pressure; J. P. Richardson; Lloyd Price; employee motivation and morale; and any other categories that seem reasonable. Don't change any words just bucket the statements."

The team of four agreed. Lloyd asked the team how it would like to deal with the new list at the next meeting. After some discussion triggered by a proposal from Jim Lowe, the team decided it would discuss each category and further clarify any of the feelings statements within them. Then, using the distributive voting process (described in this chapter), it would select the top two categories and develop some meaningful actions that would help alleviate the emotion attached to the project. For example, Richie volunteered: "Lloyd, I've talked with plenty of people the last few days in other sections, and they are at least as upset as we are. If you could just get together with the rest of J. P.'s direct reports and, as a united staff, communicate to him the intensity of all our feelings, it would make me feel a whole lot better knowing he knows. I'd feel so good, I wouldn't even quit!"

Everyone had a hearty laugh. Lloyd said: "Those are exactly the things I hope we can accomplish next time to ease us through this feelings phase. But, I want to caution everyone of you, I know J. P. well. We *are* going to have a productivity initiative for this year. He may back off a bit on his requirements if the senior staff plays its cards right in our meeting with him. But, the assignment will *not* go away; and, whatever it turns out to be, it will be on top of everything else we have to do. Our team's challenge will be to 'mine our own group gold,' so we can figure out how best to minimize the workload, pressure, and disruption this very necessary assignment brings to our operation."

The session evaluation at the end revealed a great deal of satisfaction with the meeting. A breakthrough had been made when all seemed hopeless. Just as the team was preparing to leave, Lloyd asked: "Could you hold it a second? I want to show you something. You know Peter never gave me a chance to present today's agenda. He was on me like a wildcat. But, just as an FYI, notice that, based on your e-mail and feedback, the only agenda item I had was: 'Controlled venting' with a desired outcome of 'team feelings processed.'" Ruth commented as she left with Lloyd: "I know, I know. Feelings, facts, solutions."

CHAPTER SEVEN SUMMARY

THE SEQUENCE TO GROUP PRODUCTIVITY
Feelings
Facts
Solutions

UNDERSTANDING VENTING STYLES
Expressers
Directors
Reactors
Stoics

PROCESSING FEELINGS EFFECTIVELY

Stay Neutral
- Respect people's right to have their feelings
- Encourage and acknowledge expression of feelings

Understand Rather Than Evaluate Feelings
- Probe with the nonevaluative task-oriented interpersonal behaviors
- Be sensitive to verbal and nonverbal cues

Process Feelings Using Silence, Then Flip Charts
- Silence
- Bring in the whole group
- Round-robin
- Buzz groups

Refocus the Discussion on the Original Topic and Its Desired Outcomes

Notes Worksheet: DEVELOP WRITTEN RESPONSES TO THE TWO
ITEMS LISTED BELOW

What do you feel are the main learning points from Chapter 7?	Elaborate on why you feel these points are key.

Notes

1. G. Strauss and L. Sayles, *Personnel: The Human Problems of Management* (Englewood Cliffs, NJ: Prentice-Hall, 1972), pp. 231–32.

2. L. Sayles and G. Strauss, *Human Behavior in Organizations* (Englewood Cliffs, NJ: Prentice-Hall, 1966), p. 293.

3. R. Bales, "In Conference," *Harvard Business Review* 32(2) (1954): p. 47.

4. E. Schein, *Process Consultation, Vol. II: Lessons for Managers and Consultants* (Reading, MA: Addison-Wesley, 1987), pp. 71–72.

5. Ibid.

6. A. Melcher, personal communication.

7. R. Fisher and W. Ury, *Getting to YES* (New York: Penguin Books, 1983), p. 31.

8. M. Avery, B. Auvine, B. Streibel, and L. Weiss, *Building United Judgment* (Madison, WI: The Center for Conflict Resolution, 1981), p. 73.

CHAPTER EIGHT

WORKING THE GOLD MINE: FACILITATING GROUP INTERACTION

CHAPTER OBJECTIVES

➤ To discuss proper use of the indispensable facilitation tool—the flip chart.

➤ To discuss facilitation concepts and provide tips and techniques for effective facilitation that will enhance the quality of group sessions.

INTRODUCTION

Herbert Simon, a distinguished professor of psychology at Carnegie–Mellon University and a leading force in the development of contemporary organization theory, tells a wonderful story about Louis Agassiz.[1]

When Agassiz, the great biologist, acquired a new graduate student, his first concern was to train his student to see. His standard procedure was to confront the student with a dead fish laid out on a plank and ask him or her to observe the fish until it could be described accurately. When the student, after some minutes of looking, reported to Agassiz, he or she was cross-examined thoroughly and persuaded that there were many things about the fish that the student had not seen. Agassiz sent his student back to look again, and the cycle was repeated many times. After some days, or weeks (the fish was pickled), the new graduate student finally would pass the initiation and satisfy Agassiz with his or her description. The graduate student could now see a specimen as a biologist sees it.

Like Agassiz with his graduate student, this chapter will help you see group interactions as a facilitator sees it. You will see group dynamics in a different light; you will understand how to take charge and successfully guide a group through the use of facilitation behaviors.

THE FLIP CHART: AN INDISPENSABLE TOOL

Before proceeding with the discussion on specific techniques and methods for facilitating group sessions, a word about flip charts is in order. *No group session should be conducted without flip charts!* They are the main physical tool in successful facilitation. Write on flip charts with watercolor markers that will not soak through the paper. Post flip chart pages with drafting tape, since this will not peel paint or wallpaper when it is removed.

Importance of Flip Charts. There are four significant advantages to using flip charts throughout the entire group session. Flip chart pages:

➤ Allow important data/information to be preserved and displayed during the session.

➤ Provide a common data/information base that the group can refer to and work from.

➤ Provide immediate feedback to group members that their ideas, comments, and proposals have been listened to and understood.

➤ Provide a portable postsession written record that can be given to another person for consolidation, transcription, and distribution. Or, better yet, with the proliferation of lap top computers, it is quite possible to have a participant in the session enter the flip charts as they are created. The final charts are distributed to everyone as soon as they can be sent e-mail or printed out.

Tips for Using Flip Charts.   The following ideas will help you use flip charts as an integral part of every group session.

➤ Write what people say. Don't change their words without getting their permission.

➤ Take turns being the scribe. The primary facilitator should be minimally involved with writing on the flip charts. It is difficult to scribe and be an effective facilitator at the same time. Scribing is challenging and important work. Rotate the job from time to time between two people within a given session. (This activity also can involve individuals who might appear somewhat aloof from the meeting activity.)

➤ Keep all information visible. Each time a flip chart page is filled with information, tear it off and tape it to the wall. Information recorded on a page and "flipped" over the top of the pad is essentially lost and useless for the rest of the session.

➤ When acting as scribe, make it clear to the group when you are contributing your own thoughts, ideas, and opinions. This goes back to the concept of splitting roles as discussed in Chapter 3.

➤ Summarize complicated ideas. Have people summarize their own ideas and then write their summaries.

➤ Establish a "parking lot" for values, ideas, and points worth preserving so they are not lost, but not directly related to the immediate discussion. Tear off a sheet of flip chart paper before the session begins, tape it to the wall, and label it PARKING LOT. Add group thoughts and ideas to it throughout the session. Review the parking lot periodically and use any of the information whenever it becomes relevant to the discussion. At the conclusion of the meeting, sort out which remaining pieces of information should be retained for the next session, which should be taken as action items by an individual or small subgroup to complete between this meeting and the next, and which should be dropped.

A CONCEPTUAL FRAMEWORK FOR FACILITATING A GROUP

Having planned the structure and process of a forthcoming group session, having obtained a working knowledge of the interpersonal behaviors and processes for group sessions, and having learned about the "feelings, facts, solutions" sequence, you now are in position to face the next challenge: helping the group meet the purpose and desired outcomes of the session.

Effectively facilitating a group toward achievement of its desired outcomes can seem overwhelming; and, without a framework for guiding you through the facilitation journey, it is! However, the mystery of hands-on facilitation can be reduced if the task is broken into three segments. With the session's purpose and desired outcomes already in place, effectively facilitating a group requires that you pay attention to these three primary segments:

1. *Start-up.* Warming up; initiating an open, collaborative climate.

2. *Move-out.* Proactively maintaining an open, collaborative climate; managing disruptive behaviors as required; managing confusion whenever the group gets lost; managing differences among participants; drawing conclusions at appropriate points throughout the session.

3. *Wrap-up.* Tying up loose ends and evaluating the session in order to bring it to a proper close.

165

Before moving on to discuss the set of tools, techniques, and behaviors composing each of the three phases, a link back to Chapter 7, "Feelings, Facts, Solutions," is in order. As that chapter emphasized, problem resolution—uncovering facts and developing solutions—cannot begin effectively until feelings have been properly acknowledged and resolved. The main thing for you to remember is that feelings may emerge during any of the three major segments of group facilitation. Whenever feelings arise, you must be ready and willing to stop the task-oriented activities by calling for a process check in order to help the group members work through their feelings using the techniques described in the foregoing chapter. It is quite possible that a meeting may never get into the "feelings" state. If this is the case, so much the better. Then you can concentrate on facilitating the group in working on the task without having to take time out to process feelings.

Take a few minutes now to review the model shown in Exhibit 8–1. Keyed to the different chapters in the book, this framework develops the relationship and synergy among a number of elements crucial to facilitation excellence.

1. The session's purpose and desired outcomes.
2. The three segments of any facilitation effort (start-up, move-out, wrap-up).
3. The nine primary activities within the three segments.
4. The task and maintenance behaviors plus the two gate-keeping processes.
5. The role of feelings.

The framework indicates that all three phases of facilitation—start-up, move-out, and wrap-up—always are set against a backdrop of potential feelings. As mentioned earlier, when feelings do emerge, regardless of the phase, they must be dealt with.

Exhibit 8–1 also depicts the fundamental idea that facilitating the three phases, plus facilitating feelings when necessary, always must be done with the intent of achieving the session's stated desired outcomes.

Finally, the foundation for carrying out the different activities within each of the three phases is contained in the task and

Exhibit 8-1: FACILITATING A GROUP IN THE SHARING AND PROCESSING OF INFORMATION

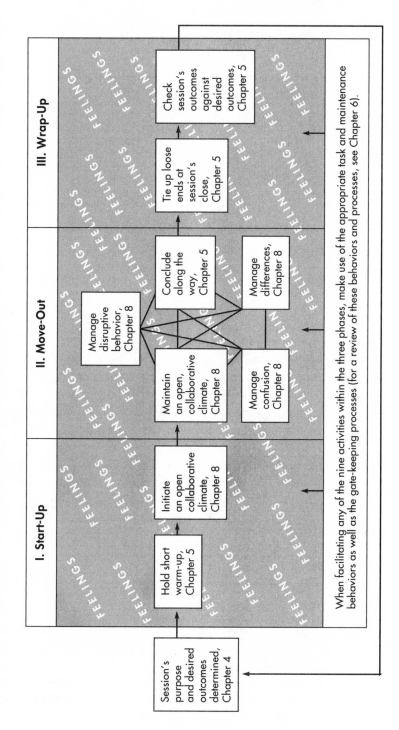

maintenance behaviors plus the gate-keeping processes. These are indicated along the bottom of the model.

INITIATING AN OPEN, COLLABORATIVE CLIMATE

You have taken the time to plan the structure and process of the forthcoming group session; your preparation is over; the team is in the conference room. Now it is time to facilitate the event. After a short warm-up, the art of excellent facilitation actually commences with the way in which the topic for discussion or analysis is presented. The manner of presentation is crucial because it sets the mood, positive or negative.[2] If process obstacles are to be avoided, you must approach each issue in a way that stresses the constructive aspects of the situation.

During the critical start-up phase, you actually are laying the foundation for a productive group session by helping group members feel comfortable so that they *want* to collaborate, and instilling in them a *need* to collaborate because the issue is recognized as important and worthy of their time and effort to work through.

Your ability to initiate an open, collaborative climate provides the crucial thrust that sets the group on course; getting off the track here will be compounded as the meeting moves onward. There are several guiding principles that can be used at this point to aid the smooth flow of a meeting and significantly reduce the chances of an emotional explosion and/or confusion, destructive conflict, or other negative situations from arising.

Present the Issue So the Focus Is on the Situation, Not on Behaviors

There are a number of sound reasons for stating the issue in situational rather than behavioral terms. To begin with, it is usually easier and less frustrating to change situations than it is to change people. Formulating and presenting an issue in terms of behaviors immediately locks in a limited and biased perspective: the *people* are to blame.

On the other hand, formulating and presenting an issue in terms of the situation immediately expands the number of possible solutions. A situational focus virtually eliminates the possibility of the "personal attack, defend, counter-attack" spiral that easily can consume and destroy a group session before it really gets underway.

Focusing on the situation does not imply that any discussion of behavior change is to be avoided. As a matter of fact, some issues—such as skill deficiencies, disruptive meeting behaviors, and disciplinary actions—only can be stated in behavioral terms. On those occasions where a behavioral focus is warranted, be sure to lock-in only on the specific behavior that needs changing; don't get into questioning the individual's attitude or personality. Be alert to, and resist, the common tendency to jump immediately to a behaviorally-oriented initial statement.

Because of its importance in generating active participation, you should work out the initial disclosure of an issue before the group session. Here is an example that demonstrates the difference between presenting an issue or problem in terms of behaviors as opposed to highlighting the situation.

The print shop of the Akron, Ohio, Central School District consistently misses deadlines. The manager of internal services could present the problem to an employee involvement team in behavioral terms by asking, "What can be done to motivate you guys to work faster?"

In situational terms, the manager could ask, "What can be done to improve the efficiency and effectiveness of our operation across our two shifts?"

Behavioral statements tend to be judgmental; they "point the finger" at group members. Situational statements are descriptive and impersonal; they seek to generate collaboration among group members—including the manager.

Present the Issue So That It Encompasses Common Interests

This guideline increases motivation among group members to embrace the issue at hand, since the effectiveness of a session is influenced by the amount of interest the issue stimulates.

169

Making the issue appealing means showing group members how they will benefit from taking a hard look at an issue or what they will gain from spending the necessary time to solve a problem. Drawing the members together by emphasizing common interests enhances the likelihood of group cooperation in reaching an acceptable solution that everyone can support. There are at least three powerful ways to present an issue so that it conveys mutual interests.

Degree of Group Control. Emphasizing the degree of control that the group has in resolving the issue is one way to demonstrate mutual interests. Even if the group is split into two or three camps, helping members realize that they have what it takes to solve the problem—or, at the very least, to develop a set of recommendations that will be given full attention by higher management—absolutely will increase the members' motivation to tackle it.

The greater the degree of control, the greater the motivation to solve the problem. Having control of one's destiny is a significant motivator. Returning to our earlier example, the internal services manager could underscore the print shop's degree of control by saying something like, "Improving the efficiency and effectiveness of the print shop is critical to our ability to service the school district. The five of you will have full access to all records. I've made certain you can talk to anyone, including the superintendent, and I've assigned Dorothy to the project to provide clerical and administrative support. Nothing is sacred about the way we've done things in the past. With 104 years of experience among you, I'm confident you can do the job. You're our best hope to lick this one."

Fairness. Another approach for creating common interests is to state the problem so it stresses fairness for all concerned. Volatile issues such as budget cuts, downsizing, reengineering, restructuring, relocation, and merit increase plans can be defused, and motivation built for a collaborative effort, if the issue emphasizes fairness.

Stress fairness with statements similar to this: "Since headquarters has mandated that our division must cut its budget by 10 percent, what would be a fair method for determining who pays what portion of the budget cut?"

Congruence Between Personal and Organizational Goals. Setting forth the issue so that personal goals are congruent with organizational goals is another technique for stimulating interest. For example, the manager could present this issue in the following manner: "The reorganization has caused a five-week slip in our schedule for the introduction of our TAK-44 model boat at the February 1 boat show. How can we recover those weeks? If we make the show, we'll get our bonus."

Initially, Share Only Primary Information

Another ingredient in building an open, collaborative climate is for you to share whatever relevant knowledge and situational facts you have regarding the topic or issue. However, in doing so, you must be careful to supply this information without interpreting it or suggesting how the information should be used. The initial information given to the group is critical, since it provides the members with their first impression of what they are undertaking.

This is not a time for hidden agendas. It is a time for honestly stating the facts so the group will have the best chance of getting off to a good start in attacking the issue. Properly supplying essential information involves several considerations.

Provide background information nonjudgmentally. Primary historical or background information must be presented in a descriptive, nonevaluative manner and without suggestions as to how the data should be used. Interpretation and evaluation comes later, when all group members, including the manager, mutually process this information.

Present only what is needed to clarify and describe the situation. This is just the beginning of the group activity. More detailed information can be introduced later in the discussion as the need arises. This prevents overwhelming the group with too much too soon.

171

Set expectations.   Alert the group members to what they should do in order to process the issue. For example, should they simply clarify the data, hold a limited discussion, provide their reactions, generate several alternatives or recommendations, hold extensive discussion and analyze the problem, solve the problem, make a decision, or do some combination of the above?

Delineate the range of freedom.   Inform the group what it can or cannot do in working the issue. This information is valuable because it provides a perspective on situational constraints and on the group's authority to act on the problem. It curbs the all too familiar situation where the group assumes it has more latitude than it actually does—and is frustrated when its actions cannot take effect.

In closing, there are no precise rules for determining the amount and type of information essential for initial sharing. You will have to make that determination based on the maturity of the group members in combination with the nature of the subject.

Be Succinct

Less is better. Use no more than five minutes to present the information called for in the three previous steps. If an incisive outline of the situation cannot be given within that time, you're probably being too long-winded. Remember, more facts and information can be added as the group session unfolds. Be brief so the group can get down to its main business: working the issue to achieve the desired outcomes.

Jean Beasley, a human resources manager in our manufacturing division, has some sound advice. "The key to being succinct is forethought. My experience indicates that many managers are prone to needlessly long descriptions of situations, issues, and problems because they are not prepared in advance to give a 'crisp' overview. Drawn-out initial comments tend to lead to only one thing: confusion. When I help managers plan meetings, I limit their initial stage-setting remarks to 250 words or less.[3]

Thus, to prevent confusion, do your planning homework, have a concise introduction of the issue prepared in advance, present it clearly and avoid attempts at restating the issue.

Wait!

To initiate a truly collaborative atmosphere, you must resist the temptation to immediately influence the thinking of the group. Using Lefton's term, the manager must avoid becoming a "promotional leader."

> A promotional leader leaks his or her own ideas to subordinates before they've had a chance to state theirs. ("I think we ought to revamp the entire plan, but right now I'd like to hear what you think.") Nothing will do more to stifle discussion and squelch candor. Once people know what the boss thinks, the whole discussion is likely to shift in the direction. . . . team leaders often use promotional leadership as a subtle means of ensuring that no real discussion takes place. They can make a show of open-mindedness, while guaranteeing that the discussion won't get out of hand. ("I'm absolutely convinced we should close down the Eureka operation, but of course we won't do it until you've had a chance to speak your minds.")[4]

Therefore, the fifth and final guideline for initiating a collaborative climate requires that you stop and hold back your thoughts, perspectives, value judgments, or favored actions.

One reason that you can have trouble holding back has to do with control. At the outset, you are in control of the session. By waiting, you are, in effect, relinquishing full control and sharing it with group members by giving them an opportunity to focus attention on areas that are important to them. The line of discussion generated by the group may be difficult for you to hear, yet these issues may be the very ones requiring debate in order to make a quality decision that the whole group can support.

From the manager's perspective, holding back does trade off total control for shared control; however, this is one of the keys to initiating a collaborative climate.

Even if you are asked for an opinion early on, you should practice the art of facilitation in a positive manner by saying something like, "Ron, I do have some thoughts as to how we can safely dispose of our hazardous wastes. However, I'm not convinced that I have THE answer. Right now, I prefer to facilitate the rest of the group to be sure everyone's ideas are heard without being influenced by my thoughts. I'll be happy to share my ideas later on, and when I do, remember that they carry no more weight than anyone else's."

As you can see from this example, the leader's views should be woven into the general group discussion as the processing of the information and data unfolds.

The recommended approach for initiating an open, collaborative climate requires that the manager introduce the issue by following the first four guidelines outlined in this section. Then, having done that, wait and keep the door open for members to freely explore the subject matter rather than restricting the discussion by imposing a specific direction to the exploration.

MAINTAINING AN OPEN, COLLABORATIVE CLIMATE

For members to willingly and constructively participate in a group session, they need to feel that their thoughts, ideas, opinions, and proposals are wanted and genuinely needed by the manager and the rest of the group members. The atmosphere must be such that everyone feels comfortable in putting his or her viewpoints on the table.

"Feeling comfortable" is not a result of participating in agreeable, superficial, flattering, frictionless meetings tending toward groupthink. Rather, it is a result of knowing one's ideas and opinions will be given a fair hearing and above all, knowing that *issues* are attacked—not people!

Group members understand that tough problems and issues require healthy debate, in-depth exploration of pros and cons, constructive criticism, disagreements, and challenges to people's positions. The leader encourages this type of participation because it is the key to the group's critical thinking.

Losing one person's contribution can be unproductive for everyone.

By being patient and using the group task functions of information seeking and opinion seeking to involve all group members, you can facilitate a great deal of interaction. As the group matures and everyone shares the responsibility for earnestly seeking out what others have to say, "mining the nuggets of wisdom" will be a rewarding experience. It also will reduce the chances of missing valuable contributions of group members.

Stimulate Contributions

Questions are the main tool for information seeking, opinion seeking, and testing comprehension. Questions are a primary force for sustaining a participative climate. Used well, questions can invigorate a group session and help drive it toward the achievement of its stated desired outcomes. Used poorly, they can stop a meeting dead in its tracks.

To stimulate and maintain collaboration, you need to ask questions that are nonthreatening yet specific enough to bring about a spirited response because they cannot be answered in just two or three words or with a curt "yes" or "no." Questions such as these are closed-ended:

"Do you think floor plan A is better than floor plan B?"

"Was organizational theory a favorite course of yours in graduate school?"

"Do you foresee a layoff in our division this year?"

Questions become threatening when they are seen by the recipient as judgmental, personality focused, or as an attempt to dig for information the person does not want to divulge. Threatening questions can be perceived as an attack; this brings about defensiveness and the possibility of a counterattack, which can destroy the session.

Frequently, threatening questions seem to press group members to reveal their own inadequacies. Most people don't like to do this, especially in a group setting.

Finally, threatening questions tend to make people feel as if they are getting the "third degree." An excellent tipoff is whether or not your questions are perceived as threatening is the guarded, clipped responses that keep coming through a succession of exchanges. The following examples show how NOT to ask questions.

"How in the hell could you have left out the conclusions section of this proposal?"

"Bruce, what excuse do you have this time for being unable to get the Lesko problem fixed once and for all?"

"Does anyone *else* have trouble understanding the three simple alternatives we are voting on?"

Good questions raise issues requiring an expansion of thought and a consideration of the situation being examined. You can produce an open-ended question that requires the receiver to elaborate on the problem or issue at hand if you non-threateningly use one of these six words: Who, What, When, Where, Why, or How.

By simply asking nonjudgmental, open-ended questions, you can orchestrate a rich and highly interactive discussion focused on achieving the desired outcomes. There are four major questioning techniques at the disposal of the group leader; all four are illustrated with examples of nonjudgmental, open-ended questions to show the potency of good questioning in maintaining an open, collaborative group session.

Direct Questions. A question aimed at a specific person to obtain his or her input to the subject being discussed. The direct question is also used for testing comprehension to ensure that the receiver has understood the content of the speaker's message.

"Dick, what do you think about slipping the schedule by 30 days?"

"Jim, we haven't heard from you yet. How does this mission statement look to you?"

"Lynn, are you saying you are not interested in an international assignment unless it is a manager's position and for a maximum of three years?"

General Address Question.   A question pitched to the whole group so that anyone can volunteer a response.

"Anyone have any ideas how we might cover those calls?"

"What do you think team; where could we cut expenses in order to fund this item?"

Return Question.   A question that is returned to the person who asked it. This is especially effective when the person asking the question appears to have more to say than the question indicates.

"Carol, you asked how to attack the problem; where would you start?"

"Stan, that's an interesting question; what is your analysis of the situation?"

Relay Question.   A question deflected to another person. An excellent technique for bringing in noncontributors or for giving the person who has the data a chance to respond directly to the question.

"Joe, you've been working in distribution for awhile; how would you respond to Sandy's question?"

"Tim, that's a tough question for me to answer; Newt, you're the financial expert, what are your views on the payback issue that Tim has raised regarding the Chadwick project?"

Recognize Constructive Participation

Another dimension critical to the maintenance of a collaborative climate is positive reinforcement of constructive participation by each member. This recognition is important because people tend to repeat behaviors that are reinforced. Recognizing members for their involvement in the group session makes it clear that participation is valued by the supervisor and that it does not go unnoticed. Essentially, positive reinforcement motivates more people to share more ideas and opinions with the whole group. With more information on the table, the group creates a more extensive database, which, in turn, increases its opportunity for building half-developed ideas into realistic solutions.

There are three useful behaviors that you need to practice routinely to increase your effectiveness in recognizing constructive participation.

Provide Reinforcement. The impact of positive reinforcement is strengthened considerably when it is communicated verbally and augmented nonverbally with expressions and gestures. Be certain, however, that the verbal message you deliver is congruent with your nonverbal cues. If not, the reinforcement is ambiguous. Studies have shown that, when faced with ambiguous messages, the receiver typically derives the meaning of the message from the nonverbal cues.

For example, if you are doodling on your pad, fidgeting in your chair, and trying to stifle a yawn while you say, "Thanks, Sylvia, for your ideas on correcting the billing problem. I appreciate your contributions; please keep sharing your suggestions with us," Sylvia will conclude that you couldn't care less about her contributions.

To provide the most credible and unambiguous positive reinforcement, you need to fortify your verbal statements with congruent expressions and gestures. The following examples illustrate the point.

➤ Verbal reinforcement: "Good," "That's right," "Thanks, that was very enlightening," "Excellent point," "You sure clarified that mess," "Well said," "Thanks, that helps," "I thing you're on the right track; tell me more."

➤ Augmented by expression: Smiling, showing a look of interest, showing a look of concentration.

➤ Augmented by gestures: Giving a positive head nod, leaning forward, giving the "A-OK" sign, giving a wave of the hand to signal the person to keep talking.

Safeguard Proposals. Every idea or proposal put forth by a group member is not going to be worthy of a detailed analysis. However, making sure that proposals and ideas are heard and understood by the whole group is a top priority for any manager attempting to mine group gold.

The value of this activity is threefold. First, it decreases the chance of prematurely rejecting an idea whose merit is not immediately obvious; second, knowing that their propositions will at least be heard and understood, it encourages group members to offer suggestions more freely; third, the group can add to an infant idea and ultimately develop it into a mature solution. Remember, a good idea doesn't care who had it!

Without protection, far too many good ideas are squashed. You constantly must be alert to the "idea killers." The difficulty in protecting proposals is that idea killers are so common that they are invoked without anyone, including the manager, ever noticing the damage being done to group productivity. Common examples of idea killers are shown below.

"That will never work."

"We've always done it this way."

"We're not ready for that yet."

"It goes against established policy."

"Don't be ridiculous!"

"It's a good idea, but . . ."

"The higher-ups will never go for it."

"Totally impractical."

"Our business is different."

"No way, not here."

"We've already tried that."

"Let's put it on the shelf for now."

"You can't be serious."

Idea killers are really death sentences for ideas—certain death for an idea that goes against the existing way of doing things. Saving ideas from being murdered by actively protecting proposals requires the facilitator to be alert for idea killers and intervene when a group member fires one across the table. The intervention should be firm, swift, and simple.

"Hold it please; before we bury Irene's proposal, let's take a few minutes to understand how it might apply."

"Let's not be too hasty; we've covered the negatives, but what about the positive aspects to Hal's idea?"

Invite Rough Proposals. This activity is closely aligned with the previous one. As facilitator, you cannot afford to have people holding back because their proposition is hazy in their own minds. If you wait for, or only accept, fully developed and well-thought-out ideas, many viable proposals and solutions may never surface. It is at times like this that you really have to "mine the group gold."

"Don't worry about not having everything buttoned up, Ann; your input is invaluable in pointing us in the right direction."

"Ryan, maybe you don't have the final answer, but we all need to hear what your idea is since it may move us that much closer to a solution."

Avoid Sustained One-on-One Interactions. Fundamental to the facilitation process is the precept that the manager facilitates a group, not one or two people. The job of the facilitator is to involve everyone present in the achievement of the group's desired outcomes. The bulk of the dialogue must be among the group members, not a sequence of one-on-one exchanges between the facilitator and two or three group members.

Getting involved in a prolonged facilitator-to-participant dialogue can sidetrack the session hopelessly, cause other members to tune out, and bias the direction of the entire session. This is especially true if the person interacting with you has a great deal of authority or influence.

You must direct the discussion in such a way that it is shared by the entire group. The following techniques help accomplish this goal.

➤ Disengage with the participant attempting a one-on-one dialogue by looking away or shifting your body position.

➤ Ask general address questions and encourage input from a variety of people.

➤ Use relay questions from you to other group members. This is an especially good technique because it breaks the participant-to-facilitator link and brings in another group member.

➤ Ask direct questions aimed at nonparticipants.

➤ Be candid; clarify your role. Say something like, "I want to take a moment to remind everybody that while I'm facilitating, my role is to stay tuned in to the group process and reduce obstacles to good group functioning. I'm not the central communication hub. I'm not heavily involved in information processing."

Should you need to add to the content of the discussion, or challenge the ideas or opinions of others, you must "switch hats" to do so, then return to the role of facilitator. Long dialogues with one or two people typically occur when you are swept up in the content of the session and forget to move back into the facilitation role to break off the discussion.

DEALING WITH DISRUPTIVE BEHAVIOR

Every meeting will have a mix of personalities. Very few sessions are comprised of people with the same behavioral characteristics; additionally, depending on the nature of the issue, its impact on each person, and a host of other factors, people vary their behavior throughout a meeting. Thus, as the session flows, an individual can move from being argumentative to quiet; another can shift from being helpful to obstructive; someone else can change from being alert and involved to withdrawn and half asleep. Two members may be upset by what happened in the previous meeting they attended; another may be preoccupied with an impending job offer. The combinations are endless.

Doyle and Straus vividly portray meeting personalities as jungle animals.

> Sometimes as you stand in front of an energetic group, you can feel as if you are standing in the middle of a jungle path with all kinds of animals rushing to a water hole. Loud, assertive beasts are pushing their way past others; sleek, speedy animals dart back and forth; timid animals wait with watchful eyes for a chance to move without being crushed. And then there are the fierce animals, more hungry rather than thirsty, ready to leap upon the unsuspecting fellow traveler.[5]

The manager, operating as group facilitator, has the task of keeping all these animals, whatever their personalities or present dispositions, working together toward the achievement of the session's desired outcomes. You should not expect, or even attempt, to change people's personalities; on the other hand, you must influence their behavior.

Experience shows that much of the disruptive behavior in group sessions is unintentional. For slight indiscretions that occur occasionally and don't put the group's effectiveness or productivity in jeopardy, the best policy is to let them slide. When a negative behavior requires confrontation, you'll have to correct the behavior without embarrassing the person, creating an uncomfortable scene, or inhibiting collaboration.

Disruptive behaviors take many forms: rambling, arguing, dominating, gate closing, side conversations, etc. These dysfunctional behaviors may occur because preparation for the group session has been inadequate. Clarification of the purpose and outcomes, along with a close rein on the agenda, can help keep the group focused on tasks and can reduce disruptive behaviors.

General Guidelines

Even with careful preparation, some troublesome behaviors may crop up. It is often possible to help difficult group members channel their energies toward more productive endeavors. Here are a few techniques to help facilitate disruptive behavior.

Firm but Friendly Confrontation.   Because much dysfunctional behavior is unintentional, dealing with the problem is not as difficult or threatening as it might seem at first glance. Many times, calling attention to the behavior in a firm but friendly manner is all that is required. To effectively confront a troublesome individual, use these methods.

➤ Zero in on the negative behaviors; do not label or classify the individual. Personal labeling raises defensiveness and provides the ingredients for an emotional explosion.

➤ Highlight the impact that the disruptive behavior is having on the group. As mentioned earlier, many times the offending person is totally unaware of the problem his or her behavior is causing the group. Once the group member is made aware of how he or she is negatively impacting the session, the individual is only too happy to stop.

➤ Suggest different, more functional, behaviors. This gives the disruptive person an easy way to save face by steering him or her in a direction that will lead to more productive contributions.

These three guidelines can be incorporated into a concise statement that confronts the offender without attacking or belittling. "Jacob, continually evaluating the group's ideas while we're brainstorming slows us down and discourages others from being totally open with their ideas. There will be plenty of time in our next session for everyone to analyze what we've come up with. Please hold your evaluations until then."

In confronting counterproductive behavior, model a direct, firm, but friendly style that group members can emulate.

Encourage Shared Responsibility for Handling Difficult Members.
In the spirit of secondary facilitation, if the group is encouraged to share the responsibility for successful facilitation, negative behaviors will decrease. Peer pressure, especially when it emanates from several different people, is a major deterrent to disruptive group behavior. Group censure puts pressure on disruptive members to modify and control their behaviors to meet the group's behavioral norms.

Use Nonverbal Cues.   Making eye contact, sending a dissatisfied glance, moving in close, placing a hand on a person's shoulder, giving a negative head nod, and stopping in mid-sentence are all ways for nonverbally communicating displeasure.

Acknowledge Acceptable Behavior.   Try to "catch the person doing something right." Disruptive behavior often is enacted to bring attention to the person; to some extent, this behavior can be altered through positive reinforcement. Watch for acceptable behavior and comment on it:

> "Excellent point, Karl. I agree we should put the artwork out for bid rather than accepting the price from our internal art services group. By the way, thanks for being on time today so you were here to share your ideas on this. If you weren't here, we might have made a costly mistake."

Research shows that people tend to repeat behaviors that are reinforced. This process takes time; you won't see a dramatic improvement in a short period.

Talk Privately with Repeat Offenders.   If these techniques fail to keep disruptive behavior from being repeated, a private conference is in order. A one-on-one discussion, where you present your concerns and the disruptive member's views are heard, provides a confidential forum to discuss feelings and needs and work out an acceptable solution. Use the firm, but friendly confrontation approach for this discussion and remember to focus on the behavior, not the personality or past history. This strategy preserves the member's sense of dignity and conserves precious session time.

Handling Specific Problems

Late Arrivers. When arriving late, some people make a grand entrance while others try to be as unobtrusive as possible. In either case, there is disruption: the door is opened, someone moves through the room, people have to clear space at the table, a jacket is removed and hung on the back of a chair, a briefcase is snapped open and shut, papers are shuffled. The momentum of the meeting has been interrupted.

If it is a rare occurrence, ignore it. Be disciplined about starting your meetings on time; build a reputation for prompt starts. If you do, people will know when you say 9:30, you mean 9:30, not 9:40 or 9:50! They will put forth a greater effort to be on time.

If the person is a chronic latecomer, don't confront him or her upon entering the room or publicly during the meeting. During a break, or after the session, ask the person why he or she is late so frequently. Don't lecture or talk down to the person. Follow the three steps of the firm, but friendly, confrontation model presented earlier.

Don't stop the meeting and review what has taken place up to that point in order to bring the latecomer up to date. This only reinforces the lateness habit: "Why be on time? I can come late and still not miss anything." Instead, simply mention the topic being discussed, point to any flip chart notes on the wall, and provide any handouts the others have. Say something like, "Sam, while you quietly review the flip charts and the handout, I'm going to continue facilitating the group discussion.

If the person is central to the information processing and a review of foregoing information is essential, call a break and do it quickly. Try to avoid using the whole group's time for the benefit of one or two people.

Talk about lateness with the whole group. See if shared values can be built around being on time. Help the group decide how it wants to deal with latecomers (many groups develop a schedule of fines based on the number of minutes late).

When a person is late for the second or third time in a row, use the silence technique. As the individual enters, pause, look at the person until he or she gets settled, and then pick up the discussion right at the point where you were interrupted.

Ramblers. The individual talks about everything except the subject, uses far-fetched analogies, gets lost. Sometimes rambling is referred to as "shooting from the lip." It steals meeting time and bores everyone. Thank the person, then refocus attention by asking the individual how his or her point(s) relate to the topic at hand. This allows for self-discovery and reduces the chance of a repeat performance.

Restate the urgency of the objectives and the time constraints. Smile and say, "Your point is interesting, but (while pointing to a flip chart, transparency, blackboard, etc.) we do seem to be a bit off the subject. We'd better get back to item three on the agenda, which has a desired outcome of . . ." Or deflect the discussion until the break by saying, "That's an interesting idea. Can you hold it until the break? We'll have more time to discuss it then. Right now, we have to cover these two remaining points."

Chronic Objectors. This person may be a combative personality, a self-appointed devil's advocate, or someone who is normally good-natured but is upset by something external to the session.

Keep your own temper firmly in check. Honestly try to find merit in one of the person's points; express your agreement, then move on to something else.

Make light of the person's remarks; don't be sarcastic, but say something like, "Well, Joel, I can see you aren't taking any hostages today!"

When a person makes an obvious misstatement, toss it to the group; ask how others feel; let them turn it down. Say something like: "How many others share Nick's view?"

Ask the person to make a positive recommendation. "Erin, you've given us a number of reasons for not recruiting at junior colleges. I'd also like to hear you present a couple of advantages."

As a last resort, talk to the person privately during a break; see if you can win the person's cooperation or uncover what the real issue is. Use the firm but friendly confrontation model presented earlier.

Dominators.   The person may be naturally garrulous or a show-off. The person also may be exceptionally well-informed and be anxious to let others know it or may be more senior than others present. If members value the contribution of the talkative one and recognize that the person's monopoly of the discussion time is temporary, there is no need to intervene.

However, dominators tend to be vocal, full of the "right" answers, and quick to jump to conclusions. Don't let them get a solid foothold in the session. If they do, they will steal "air time," intimidate some, stimulate a confrontation with others, or wage personal attacks that distract the team from its goals.

Supportively acknowledge the dominator, then immediately include another individual. Say something like, "I can understand how you feel," or "That's one view of it." Then, after making the supportive statement, actively bring in another group member, "Anna, what are your thoughts on this issue?"

Thank the person for their contribution to the issue and state you would like to hear what others in the session have to say. Say something like: "It's important to the success of this discussion that we hear from everyone in the group. Please give others a chance to share their ideas."

Gate Closers.   The person may be excited, full of ideas, or a poor listener. Most people are unaware of their gate-closing tendencies and do not do it intentionally or maliciously.

Say to the person who was gate closed, "Pam, I feel you were just shut out. Would you please continue?" Or say to the person who did the gate closing, "Gordon, please hold it a second, Archie was making his point. When he finishes, I'll get back to you." Then go back to Archie and ask him to continue.

Side Conversations.   These spring up when people in close proximity to each other feel a need to talk because they are bored, suddenly have an idea, have been repeatedly gate closed, or are excited about a point but can't get "air time."

Pause. Look at the offenders. If one of the offenders is seated nearby, place a gentle hand on the person's arm or shoulder.

Directly involve one of the talkers in the whole group discussion. Say something like, "Bob, what are some other benefits to saying open until 9:30 on Wednesday nights?"

Confront the situation directly. Say something like: "Al, Diane, could we please have one meeting? Judy has the floor."

Quiet Members. A quiet individual could be bored, indifferent, above-it-all, timid, or insecure. One person's silence can cause unrest within the group when it becomes noticeable, especially if the other group members are actively participating. Silence also is counterproductive because potentially good ideas are being withheld from the group.

If the person is bored or indifferent, arouse interest by asking for his or her opinion. Or draw out the individual next to the quiet person, then ask the quiet person to summarize the points and add his or her views on the topic.

If you're dealing with someone who feels above it all, ask for his or her input after indicating the respect the individual's experience commands. "Lenny, I know you did an awful lot of strategic planning when you worked for Putnam. How can we improve the key economic assumptions we've formulated for next year's operating plan?" However, don't overuse this technique or the rest of the group will resent it. You also can tweak this superior type by tossing a provocative query his or her way to see what reaction you get.

If a group member is timid or insecure and is sitting nearby, ask him or her a question that can be answered easily. This safely includes the quiet person and makes him or her more comfortable because the interaction is with the facilitator, not with the group as a whole. Watch for the first time a particularly sensitive person speaks up, then compliment him or her on joining the discussion. Be sincere!

Inarticulate Speakers. This individual finds it difficult to put his or her thoughts into proper words. The person has an idea but can't convey it. Assistance is required.

Don't say, "What you mean is this. . . ." Say, "Let me repeat that." (Then, put it in better language.) Bend the person's ideas only enough to have them make sense and then test comprehension by asking the person, "Did I get it right?"

Off-the-Wall Comments. This occurs when a member, often unknowingly, but sometimes for shock value, adamantly makes a statement that is obviously incorrect. Don't challenge the statement directly; this will only rev the person up and take the meeting on an unwanted tangent. Say, "I can see how you feel," or "That's one way of looking at it." Move the meeting along by stating, "Your point is an interesting one. Who else has thoughts on our 'lease-versus-buy' evaluation?"

MANAGING DIFFERENCES

Anyone who facilitates a group session will most likely be dealing with diversity. This is a normal and essential dynamic of group sessions. If all members' approaches, perspectives, and values were the same, there would be little need for group decisions at all; certainly there would be virtually no need for facilitation. The very idea of facilitation, in fact, assumes that there will be divergent ideas, opinions, and proposals for solving a common problem, reaching a goal, or making a decision.

Effectively getting the most a group has to offer requires that the manager never lose sight of a fundamental point: Conflict, in and of itself, is neither good nor bad. Whether conflict enhances critical thinking and productivity or undercuts it will depend on how you facilitate the differences at hand. In essence, your challenge is to encourage diversity without encouraging personal conflict—to harness the constructive power of differences without igniting its destructive power.

Differences as a Constructive Force

There are four good reasons for encouraging "fruitful friction" among members as they process information during a group session.

1. *Critical thinking is stimulated.* When an individual or contingent challenges the direction of a group or takes exception to an offered proposal, the group is forced to reexamine its

own beliefs in some detail and to reconsider previously ignored or skimmed over aspects of the issue.

2. *Innovation and creativity is sparked.* When people are in conflict over acceptable alternatives, this diversity can motivate the group members to work out new and creative alternatives that can be supported by everyone.

3. *Group stagnation is minimized.* Contrary opinions and ideas among group members increase the breadth and depth of each member's understanding of the subject.

4. *Healthy debate and discussion is energizing.* The excitement and energy that spring from interpersonal differences can increase the motivation and involvement of group members in tackling the task at hand.

Signs of Constructive Differences

When facilitating a discussion, what cues or signals indicate constructive differences? Above all else, high-team spirit and a mutual commitment to the desired outcomes remains center stage. The task behavior of disagreement zeros in on issues and ideas, not people. The task behaviors of testing comprehension and summarizing are used by all members to ensure that each other's viewpoints are understood—even though they may not be supported. Participants respond to what others actually are saying, not to what they think others are saying. The discussion stays on the topic and contributes to the attainment of the desired outcomes. Finally, members see the time and energy spent discussing and modifying differing ideas and alternatives as worthwhile because this effort produces results that are better than any one individual could produce alone.

Differences as a Destructive Force

Disagreements and differences are destructive when they paralyze the group's ability to realize its desired outcomes. There are four reasons why you cannot tolerate destructive interpersonal conflict.

1. *"Winners" are produced at the expense of "losers."* Win/lose is individual selfishness manifesting itself in a group. People's energies are directed toward each other in an adversarial atmosphere of total victory versus total defeat. Implementation of "the winning decision" is a constant struggle or, in some cases, even impossible because of the active or passive resistance that the "losers" creatively employ.

2. *Polarization is fostered.* In a destructive mode, conflict does not produce, "fruitful fiction." Instead, opposing opinions cause members to defend their ideas rather than modify them. "Getting my own way" becomes more important than discovering the ramifications of, and solution for, the group's current dilemma.

3. *Energy is consumed unproductively.* Preparing for battle takes time and effort. In addition, alternately defending one's own position and attacking the opponent's stance in the heat of controversy drains energy from the combatants. This energy is being siphoned off in an internal "we–they" fight rather than being harnessed in a cooperative undertaking of "us against the problem."

4. *A short-term orientation takes hold.* At the destructive level, group members become conflict-oriented (stressing the here-and-now differences) as opposed to being relationship-oriented (accentuating the long-term consequences of their differences and the methods of resolving them).

Signs of Destructive Differences

There are telltale indications that the discussion is headed toward destructive conflict, just as there are signs of constructive controversy when it is occurring. The clearest and most common signal that the meeting is self-destructing is when a number of members start resorting to personal attacks instead of focusing on the facts and issues. This, in turn, produces a whole series of attack/defend spirals that rob the session of its productivity. Likewise, emotionally charged one-upsmanship or the same negative statements being presented again and again by the same people should alert you to the possibility of unmanaged and ruinous conflict. Members not listening to what others are saying but reacting to what they *think* others are saying, and members digging in with unyielding attachment to their own ideas are two other sure signs of destructive differences.

Effectively Managing Differences

The key to effectively managing differences is to first understand where people are coming from and then work to resolve areas of diversity. Differences frequently seem bigger than they really are because in collaborative group sessions, a lot of time is spent discussing different viewpoints and disagreements. Often the group loses sight of both the common goals and areas where there is agreement. The following process can help correct the situation by fostering consensus.

Clarify Points of View.   Start with a period of silence so people can collect their thoughts. Then summarize all of the points of view on a flip chart. As each one is written down, check back with the originator to be sure the statement is accurate. It's possible to have as many different viewpoints as there are members in the group; however, the more common occurrence is to have conflict among several subgroups of people who share common viewpoints. Stay away from positions. Get people to talk about their interests, what are they interested in achieving and why.

Define Areas of Agreement.   Ask members to read all the statements and help itemize the areas of agreement or synergy among interests. The scribe compiles a list of the areas of agreement on flip chart paper as the group develops them. Give verbal recognition to any person who demonstrates clear thinking and/or leadership during the agreement definition activity.

As an aid to effectively carrying out this exercise, the following checklist can be used as a starting point to uncover common areas for agreement.

➤ **Goals:** Is there agreement on what end result the group is trying to accomplish?

➤ **Roles:** Is there agreement on who can or should do what?

➤ **Procedures:** Is there agreement on the methods or approach used for doing things (accomplishing goals, resolving issues, solving problems, making decisions, etc.)?

➤ **Relationships:** Is there agreement on what is or is not possible?

➤ **Limits:** Is there agreement on how the people will relate to each other?

➤ **Timing:** Is there agreement on when things should be accomplished or decided?

This is not an exhaustive list; therefore, the group should add other areas it feels are important. The main task, however, is to search for agreements or synergy among several interests, no matter how simple.

Define Areas of Disagreement. Next, ask the group to sort out and clarify the major points of disagreement among the stated interests. These are noted on a flip chart by the scribe.

Specifying the points of contention advances everyone's understanding of the situation because then they can see the "essence of the difference." It makes the disagreement more objective by moving it out of feelings, subjectivity, and emotionalism. Also, defining the areas of disagreement moves the problem from the realm of something nebulous and unmanageable to the realm of something of substance that is manageable.

Use the same list of common areas (goals, roles, procedures, etc.) given above as a focal point for defining areas of disagreement. For example, it may become evident that while the group is in agreement about what end result they are interested in accomplishing (goal), who is to do what (roles), and what is and is not possible (limits), the group is not in agreement about the specific methods for accomplishing the goals (procedures), nor are they in agreement on when key decisions need to be made (timing).

This process makes it much easier to understand and resolve a difference because the issue has been stripped to the bone.

Take Steps to Resolve the Differences. With the differences plainly articulated, you can engage the group in the task of finding the sources of the differences. For example, have they arisen because of disparate facts, conflicting priorities, contrary values, divergent assumptions, or something else?

Once the sources have been identified, the group should set about resolving the least important differences first, in order to gain momentum and confidence that the differences can be resolved. Don't waste in-session meeting time trying to resolve differences extraneous to the group discussion. Set those aside and handle them outside the session.

REDUCING CONFUSION

Groups can get lost in the problems they try to solve. At any time during the processing of information, a group can become confused about what the real issues are, where the group is headed, what it is trying to decide, and the like. A course of action that is clear and simple to three members may be fuzzy and complex to seven others. On occasion, the entire group may have difficulty locating its position after it has decided where it wants to go and has begun the journey to get there. In these instances, the facilitator will have to intervene and deal with the group's impending disarray.

Confusion is a serious problem in groups because of the relationship between people's self-orientation and their feelings. Some people feel uncertain and anxious if they don't know where they are. Others may feel they are making no progress when, in fact, they are. Still others may feel they are adrift on a sea of muddled thinking.

Confusion has a debilitating effect on group productivity; you should step in to restore focus and direction whenever you sense that the discussion is going around in circles or is splintered in several directions. Verbal cues such as, "What are we discussing?" "What are we trying to decide?" or "What is the objective of this discussion?" are clear signals that it's time to reorient the group.

To reduce confusion, use the maintenance behavior of performance checking and stop the group activity. This allows the group members to pause and concentrate their attention on affirming what they are attempting to do and clarifying what they are *not* trying to do.

There are two types of confusion that clutch a group. *Type 1 confusion* arises when the group, after determining its desired outcomes and starting on the journey to get there, loses sight of what it originally set about to accomplish. *Type 2 confusion* materializes when the group gets entangled in the various processes and procedures it is trying to use.

Type 1: "Where Are We Going?"

The cornerstone for managing this type of confusion is to have clearly defined desired outcomes. Make certain that every discrete topic on the agenda has its own desired outcomes, which should be written on flip chart pages, understood by all participants, and posted for all to see.

By setting in place an agreed-upon reference point that describes where the group wants to be after working through a particular topic, you have a focal point to refer to at any time when it is necessary to remind participants of the desired outcomes and put a drifting discussion back on course. If outcomes are clearly stated and posted, Type 1 confusion can be eliminated in almost every case.

Occasionally, due to the nature of the information being shared and processed, the group may decide to alter its course part way through the discussion. Then you should call for a performance check to get the group to redefine the desired outcomes and post them for future reference.

Type 2: "What Should We Be Doing?"

Once a group has decided on its destination, it can become so involved in getting there that it gets lost on the way. When the

195

group becomes entangled in the processes it is using to solve a problem, you need to temporarily halt the activity with a performance check.

After calling for a time out, ask each person to state what he or she thinks the group should or should not be doing. As thoughts are volunteered, the information is written on a flip chart (see Exhibit 8–2).

Once all the statements are captured on flip chart pages and posted for everyone to review, specific questions (especially those of clarification) are taken up regarding any of the items. This clarifying step is needed to ensure group understanding of the information on both lists.

When the statements are clear, the whole group examines both lists and identifies any items that are the same and appear in both lists. Those that are included on both sides need to be discussed by the entire group. By mutual consent, the group decides on which side of the chart the item belongs. Put brackets around the duplicate item that is eliminated.

Finally, the points on the "should be working on" list are summarized to refocus the group.

For many facilitators, facing up to wheel spinning and working with the group to remedy it can appear to be an impossible task. Attempting to reduce confusion without a road map will demonstrate that a great deal of time can be consumed with nothing to show for the effort. Recognizing which type of confusion the group is dealing with and taking the actions recommended here will greatly diminish the burden of reducing group confusion.

CLOSING COMMENT

The techniques presented in this chapter are intended as guides; they are not rigid prescriptions. Some techniques may come naturally to you, while others may require more practice and work. There is nothing magical about them; it's simply a matter of trying them and assessing how things went, making modifications wherever appropriate, and then practicing the behaviors again. As in earlier chapters, the chapter summary and "Notes Worksheet" conclude Chapter 8.

Exhibit 8–2: KEEPING YOUR GROUP PROCESS ON TRACK

Our Group SHOULD be Working on . . .	Our Group SHOULD NOT be Working on . . .
Which category of solutions looks best right now	*[How the selected criteria will be weighted]*
Which criteria we will use to select a final solution	*How to implement the solution*
How the selected criteria will be weighted	*Making a final decision on which solution to implement*
etc.	*etc.*
etc.	*etc.*

CHAPTER EIGHT SUMMARY

THE FLIP CHART: AN INDISPENSABLE TOOL

Importance of Flip Charts
- FC pages allow important information to be preserved and displayed
- FC pages provide a common information base for group to work from
- FC pages provide immediate feedback that information has been listened to and understood
- FC pages provide a portable post-session written record that can be given to another person for transcription and distribution

Tips for Using Flip Charts
- Write what people say
- Take turns being the scribe
- Keep all information visible
- When acting as scribe, make it clear when you are adding your own thoughts
- Summarize complicated ideas
- Establish and use a "parking lot"

A CONCEPTUAL FRAMEWORK FOR FACILITATING A GROUP

Start-up

Move-out

Wrap-up

INITIATING AN OPEN, COLLABORATIVE CLIMATE

Present the Issue So the Focus Is on the Situation, Not on Behaviors

Present the Issue So That It Encompasses Common Interests
- Degree of group control
- Fairness
- Congruence between personal and organizational goals

Initially, Share Only Primary Information
- Provide background information nonjudgmentally
- Present only what is needed to clarify and describe the situation
- Set expectations
- Delineate the range of freedom

Be Succinct

Wait!

MAINTAINING AN OPEN, COLLABORATIVE CLIMATE

Stimulate Contributions
- Direct question
- General address question
- Return question
- Relay question

Recognize Constructive Participation
- Provide reinforcement
- Safeguard proposals
- Invite rough proposals
- Avoid sustained one-on-one interactions

DEALING WITH DISRUPTIVE BEHAVIOR

General Guidelines
- Firm but friendly confrontation
- Encourage shared responsibility for handling difficult members

- Use nonverbal cues
- Acknowledge acceptable behavior
- Talk privately with repeat offenders

Handling Specific Problems
- Late arrivers
- Ramblers
- Chronic objectors
- Dominators
- Gate-closers
- Side conversations
- Quiet members
- Inarticulate speakers
- Off-the-wall comments

MANAGING DIFFERENCES

Differences as a Constructive Force
- Critical thinking is stimulated
- Innovation and creativity is sparked
- Group stagnation is minimized
- Healthy debate and discussion is energizing

Signs of Constructive Differences
- High-team spirit
- Commitment to desired outcomes
- Issues attacked, not people
- Testing comprehension and summarizing used to enhance understanding
- Members responding to what is said, not what they think is said
- Discussion focuses on achievement of desired outcomes
- Time spent working through issues is seen as well spent

Differences as a Destructive Force
- "Winners" produced at expense of "losers"
- Polarization is fostered
- Energy is consumed unproductively
- Short-term orientation takes hold

Signs of Destructive Differences
- Personal attacks
- Attack/defend spiral

- Same negative statements repeated over and over
- Members responding to what they think is said, not what actually is said
- Members digging in with attachment to own ideas
- Emotionally charged one-upsmanship

Effectively Managing Differences
- Clarify points of view
- Define areas of agreement
- Define areas of disagreement
- Take steps to resolve the differences

REDUCING CONFUSION

Type 1: "Where Are We Going?"

Type 2: "What Should We Be Doing?"

Notes Worksheet: DEVELOP WRITTEN RESPONSES TO THE TWO
ITEMS LISTED BELOW

What do you feel are the main learning points from Chapter 8?	Elaborate on why you feel these points are key.

Notes

1. A. J. Melcher, *Structure and Process of Organizations: A Systems-Approach* (Englewood Cliffs, NJ: Prentice-Hall, 1976), x.

2. This section builds on the classic work of N. R. F. Maier, *Problem-Solving Discussions and Conferences: Leadership Methods and Skills* (New York: McGraw-Hill, 1963), pp. 74–97. See also F. C. Miner, Jr., who presents his Problem Centered Leadership (PCL) research findings in the article "A Comparative Analysis of Three Diverse Decision Making Approaches," *Academy of Management Journal* 22(1) (1979): pp. 81–93.

3. J. Beasley, personal communication.

4. R. E. Lefton, "Communication: The Eight Barriers to Teamwork," *Personnel Journal,* January 1988, p. 18.

5. M. Doyle and D. Straus, *How to Make Meetings Work,* (New York: The Berkley Publishing Group, 1976), p. 105.

CHAPTER NINE

MINING GROUP GOLD WITH TECHNOLOGY: THE EMERGENCE OF COMPUTER SUPPORTED MEETINGS

CHAPTER OBJECTIVES

➤ To understand how technology is beginning to affect group sessions.

➤ To describe the benefits and drawbacks of computer supported meetings.

➤ To provide a set of hints for successful computer supported meetings.

INTRODUCTION

Every day each of us gets a little splashed, if not fully soaked, as wave after wave of new technology washes across our daily lives. From the automatic teller machine, to the pay-at-the-pump gas station, to the personal computer, we all experience the effects of technological change. Some of us exult in the progress it brings; others of us stubbornly resist each and every intrusion on our traditional way of doing things.

Technological developments introduce seemingly radical changes; yet, at the same time, certain proven principles of fact and experience hold steady and continue to operate as the bedrock for the new technology. The ability to synthesize new opportunities of today with sound principles of the past helps reduce our fear of the unknown so we can learn to use a new technology to its maximum advantage. For instance, access to an automatic teller machine in no way suspends our responsibility to prudently manage our personal budget, but it can make our banking task more convenient and extend greater flexibility and freedom to our lives.

Collaborative work sessions are no different. While the vast bulk of meetings throughout the world will continue to be conducted in the traditional manner for many years to come, there can be no denying that technology will have an increasing effect on group processes in the future. But, even as hardware and software gain greater acceptance in group settings, the underlying principles for maximizing their impact on teamwork and collaboration will not radically change. The principles essentially will be the same ones I've stressed throughout this book; they will be the common link between the old and the new.

CATEGORIES OF GROUP INTERACTION

Groupware is the common name given to meeting hardware and software tools. Just as technology has revolutionized the way organizations and individuals perform their work, new groupware is continually being created to increase the productivity of teams as they work together on their day-to-day jobs and on special improvement projects. Johansen has classified group work into four categories built across the dimensions of place and time.[1] Using Johansen's dimensions, a matrix can be developed as shown in Exhibit 9–1 that highlights and labels the four categories.

Technology is currently being developed and applied across all four categories of group work. While all four are interesting, it is the "face-to-face" category of groupware which ties directly to the collaborative practices addressed throughout

Exhibit 9–1: GROUP INTERACTION CATEGORIES

	Same Place	Different Place
Same Time	**Face-to-Face** PC projectors, copyboards, decision rooms, polling systems	**Networked** PicTel conferences, on-line networks, satellite downlinks
Different Time	**Single Point** Team "war" rooms, shared workstations, group displays	**Distributed** Voice mail, e-mail, group writing and editing

Mining Group Gold. Our focus will be on an emerging type of process software designed explicitly to help group members be more productive as they gather together inside the four walls of a conference room.

The leading example of "same time, same place" meeting software is *MeetingRight*™, a meeting process software package developed by the Xerox Corporation. *MeetingRight*™ was directly modeled on the principles and practices established in *Mining Group Gold* and was piloted for some five years by close to a thousand Xerox teams. Today, *MeetingRight*™ is a commercially available Windows application product.[2]

OPERATION OF "SAME TIME, SAME PLACE" GROUPWARE

"Same time, same place" groupware such as *MeetingRight*™ is designed to support all meetings in which participants interact to share information, develop ideas, process recommendations, plan projects, reach agreements, or make decisions. In effect, this groupware supports any general purpose staff meeting or specific team improvement session. To be used effectively, it requires a liquid crystal display panel or other projection hardware.

A *technical facilitator* (TF) is required to navigate the software and assist the manager, task-force chairperson, team leader— or whomever is designated as primary facilitator—in several other activities: (1) planning the meeting; (2) managing the agenda and recording key information during the meeting; and (3) producing professionally formatted meeting minutes immediately upon completion of the session. The role and relationship of the technical facilitator (TF) to the work session is critical and will be covered under "Hints for Successful Computer Supported Meetings." As you'll soon see, the capabilities of the software align very closely with the techniques and principles detailed earlier in Chapters 4 and 5.

Pre-Meeting Activities

The technical facilitator (TF) meets with the person calling the session (i.e., the primary facilitator) in order to plan the meeting. Specifically, the TF records on a "Meeting Information" computer screen the name, location, date, start time, and purpose of the meeting. The TF also notes any pre-reading or other required materials along with any special circumstances relating to the meeting. On a separate "Participant Information" screen, the TF lists the names, organizations, phones, and addresses of all meeting participants and assigns meeting roles to each. Finally, the TF works with the primary facilitator to build a detailed agenda for the meeting. This includes determining the specific leaders for the various items on a multi-topic agenda, planning the time and desired outcome for each agenda topic, and designating each topic as either an "information sharing" or an "information processing" event. All this information is neatly formatted as a "Meeting Notice" and distributed to all participants to inform and promote effective preparation for the meeting.

In-Session Activities

The TF uses the software to carry the burden of scribe, minute-taker, and timekeeper for the meeting. Separate computer

206

screens are employed to record important notes, action items, key issues, agreements, and an agenda item summary for each topic. When needed, the TF can call up the electronic brainstorming utility to assist the team in listing, reducing, and ranking ideas, and in displaying the results as fishbone or pareto diagrams.

Throughout the meeting, the TF uses the data and warning messages from the electronic timekeeper to remind the team of its progress against the agenda and to optimize the use of team time. Finally, the TF facilitates the team in performing an evaluation of the group's meeting effectiveness by using either the "Meeting Assessment" screen for free-form positive and negative comments or the "Discussion Assessment Survey" screen to rate performance against nine critical meeting criteria.

The TF also can collaborate with meeting participants to integrate other Windows-compatible software applications into the flow of the meeting. As each agenda topic is addressed, the TF projects other electronic documents such as Powerpoint presentations and Excel spreadsheets whenever needed to optimize achievement of the desired outcomes. As other applications are presented and discussed, the TF makes on-line revisions to them and records additional notes in the appropriate computer screens.

Post-Session Activities

At the end of the group session, the TF prints and distributes professionally formatted meeting minutes. Each member leaves the room with accurate and current meeting information including individual action items.

BENEFITS OF "SAME TIME, SAME PLACE" GROUPWARE

What makes all of this different from a traditional meeting? What are the compensating benefits for buying, learning, and using all this new technology? The main difference is an overlay of additional productivity beyond what is already achievable

207

from the routine use of effective meeting principles. The electronic technology builds on the core principles of *Mining Group Gold*. It does what automation has always done best: It enhances meeting organization and eliminates drudgery by providing speed and flexibility. By assisting with the mechanical routines of the session's structure, the manager and team members are more free to concentrate on the facilitation of interpersonal behaviors, content processing, feelings issues, consensus building, and the like. Similar to the gift of power steering to the motorist, electronic technology relieves the team members from much of the manual strain of maneuvering the vehicle and allows them to focus on getting where they desire to go.

Improved Pre-Session Planning

Automated support builds in greater discipline to develop a clear meeting purpose and desired outcomes, set agenda clock times, determine the topic leaders, and outline requirements for prework. As stated in Chapter 4, all of this helps optimize the use of human resources. Thoughtfully developed "Meeting Notices" ensure only appropriate people come to the meeting and that participants come prepared to conduct specific business with defined outputs.

Improved In-Session Processing

Projected on-screen electronic meeting technology harnesses the capability of the group by creating a single point of visual focus. In addition to speaking and hearing, meeting participants now see key ideas, agreements and actions composed on-line. Visual reinforcement of critical thoughts, combined with the ability to quickly and neatly modify and expand them, engages the collective power of the group.

Ideas which might otherwise have been left incomplete or only partially understood are easier to clarify, refine, and condense. Creativity can be enhanced by automated brainstorming, grouping of ideas, weighted voting, and charting.

Action items are simpler to ferret out and discuss to ensure feasibility and commitment. In the hands of a good technical facilitator, in-session meeting technology encourages all participants to contribute to the group effort and to feel committed to the results.

Enhanced Between-Meeting Productivity

At the end of a computer supported meeting, participants receive a set of neatly formatted minutes containing immediately recognizable results which they have participated in creating. The opportunity for effective use of time until the next session is significantly increased due to enhanced teamwork and the power of effective documentation. There is no delay or confusion over what needs to be accomplished by next time.

Transparent Training

In addition to the productivity that comes from effectively processing issues and reaching agreement on outputs, computer supported meetings, when used well, have the ability to reinforce and extend the effects of traditional training. By following the logic of software generated screens designed to prompt positive behaviors, participants can change their attitudes and raise their expectations regarding group session productivity.

People acquainted with meeting software find themselves gradually internalizing core principles of how to mine group gold and then transferring this knowledge back and forth between both traditional and technology assisted sessions. The technology reinforces the power of group sessions and, when used widely in an organization, has the potential to accelerate cultural change.

Organizational Learning

High quality meeting information is instantly generated and preserved for use by participants and others throughout the organization who have a need to know. The implications for organizational development is potentially profound. By consistently and flexibly supporting the core principles of effective meetings, by transparently reinforcing effective behaviors, and by producing immediate, clear and condensed documentation, software supported meetings can leverage productivity and accelerate organizational learning.

BARRIERS TO "SAME TIME, SAME PLACE" GROUPWARE

Anyone trying to capture the opportunities offered by computer supported meetings will have to deal with some inevitable barriers. Understanding what they are and why they exist is the first step to overcoming them.

Resistance to Change

As we have seen, software supported meetings represent a force for improved productivity. But improvement requires change, and change—social, technological, behavioral, or otherwise—often is resisted. We all know and understand the status quo. We might not always enjoy it, but its familiarity makes it preferable to the unknown consequences of the new order of things. Visionary leaders and change agents see beyond the immediate discomfort to the bigger payoffs. For most people, however, acceptance comes only after familiarity with demonstrated successes and initial positive personal experiences.

Not Knowing or Valuing the Basic Principles of *Mining Group Gold*

While meeting technology certainly represents change, all of the resistance is not triggered by the new software and hardware. Poorly conceived and conducted traditional meetings will not be improved simply by bringing in a technical facilitator, a computer, and the latest meeting software. If participants have not yet assimilated, practiced and committed to the principles, techniques, and processes of *Mining Group Gold,* or if they are not enthusiastic about using the software, employing advanced technological tools will not help. To paraphrase an old adage: Technology cannot make a "silk meeting" out of a sow's ear.

Buying and Learning to Use New Equipment

Software is not free. Dollars for capital equipment like computers and projection systems can be especially hard to find in times of tight budgets, and the approval processes for such investments can be difficult and bureaucratic. Once acquired, equipment operation must be learned. Even participants not directly responsible for using the hardware can be annoyed or intimidated by the process of setting up temporary equipment, routing wires and coupling connectors. By setting up equipment in advance, smart—and courteous—technical facilitators avoid subjecting meeting participants to any technical gymnastics and meeting delays. The good news is, as time goes by, equipment prices will continue to drop while computer acceptance and literacy in the work environment will continue to grow.

Modifying the Meeting Room

Most traditional meeting rooms require some physical adjustments before they can properly support electronic meetings. Casual observers can quickly agree on what needs to be done, but unless someone takes the lead, the changes won't get made. A primary improvement includes horseshoe-shaped table arrangements with one or two projection screens. The optimal setup uses two screens. This accommodates simultaneously exhibiting information from the computer generated liquid crystal projector while showing transparencies on a regular overhead projector. The other key room modification is more flexible illumination to allow clear projection while providing enough light for participants to read, take occasional private notes, and interact across the table. If people's

211

visual needs are not met, they will blame the technology and resist its use.

Navigating the Software

The complexity of software applications can vary tremendously. Even the most straightforward applications require a period of familiarization; private practice is imperative. A team quickly will be turned off by a TF learning on-the-fly how to navigate the computer screens and keystroke the information. Individual fear of learning the software and then having to use it in front of the group can be a barrier to acceptance of the technology. Lack of reasonable keyboarding skills also can be an impediment. Using a trained, third party TF to support initial meetings and to provide live, in-session coaching to meeting members is a recommended solution.

HINTS FOR SUCCESSFUL "SAME TIME, SAME PLACE" COMPUTER SUPPORTED MEETINGS

Hints for the Primary Facilitator

Lead the charge for change. Successful change occurs faster within an organization when sponsored and role modeled by its influential people—both managers and non-managers. Enthusiasm for computer supported sessions will come about only if some of the influential people endorse the concept through both words and actions. These opinion shapers, operating as visible primary facilitators need to: (1) personally invest in understanding the new tools; (2) communicate the benefits and expectations to the group; (3) encourage participants' support and patience with their own learning curve; (4) applaud positive results and appropriate behavioral changes; and, (5) continue to explore all the capabilities of the new technology.

Select the right technical facilitator. The desired state for a progressive group would be to integrate the technology into its meeting processes and develop its own internal technical capability. Still, depending on its level of proficiency in meeting practices and its comfort with technical tools, a team may find it needs help to get started. Therefore, it is not unusual for many teams to require a third party to facilitate the software. In fact, for teams that meet irregularly, or are cross-functional and of limited duration, or meet in formal settings, use of an outside TF can become a standard practice. Engaging an outsider allows all members to concentrate on practicing the behaviors fostered by the software and taking charge of the flow and content of the meeting. Over time, the role of technical facilitator can gradually be assumed by one or several group members.

The TF role is not, by any stretch of the imagination, a trivial, robotic one. It requires knowledge, skill, patience, and understanding. Therefore, in selecting a technical facilitator for a particular session, the primary facilitator should seek someone with a good balance of the following attributes:

➤ *Computer literacy:* can load and manipulate software applications and files.

➤ *Data entry skills:* can keyboard with moderate speed and reasonable accuracy.

➤ *Listening and reasoning skills:* can listen attentively and extract key ideas, issues, and agreements from spoken dialogue.

➤ *Language skills:* can draft clear, grammatical prose and make on-line edits in response to participants' comments.

➤ *Interpersonal skills:* can work constructively as a guide and support to the group without intruding on other participants' roles and responsibilities.

Be an *active* primary facilitator. Once a TF has been designated, the primary facilitator simply has found a critical support person, not a surrogate for his or her own joint role as formal leader of the team (contributing fully to content) and primary facilitator (focused on team processes). The TF, relying on the

213

software to carry the mechanical burden, should be expected to assume the multiple roles of scribe, minute-taker, and timekeeper. The primary facilitator remains responsible for the overall planning and conduct of the session, including the successful integration of the new technology into the group's work practices.

This means the primary facilitator must collaborate with the TF before the event to provide all the information necessary to complete the "Meeting Notice." It also means coordinating closely with the TF during the meeting to guide progress and behaviors consistent with the intelligent use of the software to optimize meeting results. At the session's conclusion, some primary facilitators like to review the minutes of the meeting with the TF in detail to ensure accuracy and completeness before distribution to the participants and an extended audience. This activity is a matter of personal choice.

Hints for the Technical Facilitator

Define your role. When computer technology is first introduced into a meeting, the TF is clearly critical to its successful use. This person becomes a lightening rod for the participants' curiosity and uncertainty about this "new fangled technology." How does the software work? What changes will it require? What exactly is the TF supposed to be doing for the group?

The simple, straightforward answer to the above questions is that the TF serves as the interface to the technology. And, since the technology automates scribing, minute taking, and timekeeping, the TF assumes these three traditional meeting roles. Communicating this role before beginning the session will clarify how the TF and the software work in tandem to improve the team's meeting productivity.

Translate, don't transcribe. The technology changes the TF's scribing role somewhat from the traditional manual one. Keyboarding gives the TF considerable speed and flexibility in recording more extensive meeting notes. However, this increased speed and flexibility can be a deadly trap if it leads to an attempt to record full transcriptions of the group's dialogue. The TF is not a Congressional stenographer trying to capture every word for the *Congressional Record*.

The true value of a skilled TF comes from that person's ability to extract the essence of the ongoing dialogue and present it briefly and clearly on the projection screen for the group's approval, disagreement, refinement, or major modification. By providing the summarized highlights of the information sharing and processing, the technical facilitator presents a continuous "picture" of what is being said. This prompts the participants to focus on mining their group gold real time. This dynamic process helps deliver improved clarity, consensus, and commitment to learn results.

Continually test comprehension.   Just as the manual scribe has the *power of the pen*, the electronic scribe has the *power of the keyboard* to capture the thinking of the group. It is a power that must never be abused. An excellent scribe—manual or electronic—must have excellent listening skills. The TF's main weapon against abusing the power of the keyboard is the interpersonal behavior of testing comprehension—asking for feedback on the written notes. Comments like "Have I captured what you've been saying?", "Did I get this right?", or "Is this what you mean?" all serve to ensure each team member is being heard and understood. With the correct base of information being laid down, important additions and modifications can be triggered.

Guide, don't decide.   The effective TF guides the group to clarity through repeatedly employing the interpersonal behaviors of seeking information and opinions, summarizing, testing comprehension, and supporting. The TF stops far short of substituting his or her judgment for that of the group members. All decisions on content or phrasing of notes, action items, or any aspect of the meeting process itself always remains the exclusive prerogative of the primary facilitator and the session participants.

215

Hints for Meeting Participants

Focus on the messages, don't wordsmith. Meeting members committed to improving their session's productivity will adjust to the role of the TF. They will routinely browse the projected screens scanning and responding to the TF's notes. Effective team members also make a distinction between proposing useful changes in content and meaning and requiring arbitrary wording changes that are not value added to the resulting messages. Detailed wordsmithing that does not substantially affect achievement of the session's desired outcomes is unproductive and quickly detracts from the net benefits of using meeting software tools.

Continually practice secondary facilitation. When new technology is introduced into a group's meetings, some participants, often unconsciously, reduce their level of involvement while they orient themselves to the new tools. Although this behavior is normal, it is important that it be short-lived. Just as in traditional meetings, each participant carries an obligation to contribute substantively to the content, to positively shape the process and mood of the session, and to employ constructive use of both the task and maintenance interpersonal behaviors. In short, secondary facilitation is just as much a requirement in technology-based sessions as it is in traditional sessions. Technology can help leverage these behaviors to improve productivity, but it is not a substitute for them.

In summary, I'm certain that "mining group gold with technology" is something that will gain in popularity as we leave the twentieth century and enter the twenty-first. "Same time, same place" groupware technology is an important contribution to the advancement of interpersonal productivity. However, any technology is only an electronic tool and, by itself, is not capable of turning "meeting lead" into "meeting gold." The foundation principles of mining group gold will always be the timeless bedrock of group session effectiveness regardless of the format—be it traditional- or technology-based. Still, don't overlook the potential productivity improvements to your team sessions through the proper use of "same time, same place" groupware.

CHAPTER NINE SUMMARY

CATEGORIES OF GROUP INTERACTION
Face-to-Face
Networked
Single Point
Distributed

OPERATION OF "SAME TIME, SAME PLACE" GROUPWARE

Pre-Meeting Activities

In-Session Activities

Post-Session Activities

BENEFITS OF "SAME TIME, SAME PLACE" GROUPWARE

Improved Pre-Session Planning

Improved In-Session Processing

Enhanced Between-Meeting Productivity

Transparent Training

Organizational Learning

BARRIERS TO "SAME TIME, SAME PLACE" GROUPWARE

Resistance to Change

Not Knowing or Valuing the Basic Principles of *Mining Group Gold*

Buying and Learning to Use New Equipment

Modifying the Meeting Room

Navigating the Software

HINTS FOR SUCCESSFUL "SAME TIME, SAME PLACE" COMPUTER SUPPORTED MEETINGS

Hints for the Primary Facilitator
- Lead the charge for change
- Select the right technical facilitator
- Be an active primary facilitator

Hints for the Technical Facilitator
- Define your role
- Translate, don't transcribe
- Continually test comprehension
- Guide, don't decide

Hints for Meeting Participants
- Focus on the messages, don't wordsmith
- Continually practice secondary facilitation

Notes Worksheet: DEVELOP WRITTEN RESPONSES TO THE TWO
ITEMS LISTED BELOW

What do you feel are the main learning points from Chapter 9?	Elaborate on why you feel these points are key.

Notes

1. See: R. Johansen, D. Sibbet, S. Benson, A. Martin, R. Mittman, P. Saffo, *Leading Business Teams: How Teams Can Use Technology and Group Process Tools to Enhance Performance* (Reading, MA: Addison-Wesley Publishing Company, 1991), pp. 15–22.

2. Information on *MeetingRight*™ meeting effectiveness software and *SolvingRight*™ group problem solving software can be obtained from Xerox Quality Services.

For more information about Xerox training and consulting on a comprehensive range of quality topics, please contact:

Xerox Quality Services

PO Box 20423

Rochester, NY 14602–9898

1-800-438-5077

CHAPTER TEN

"Let's Have a Team-Building Session!" An Integrative Case Study

CHAPTER OBJECTIVES

➤ To use an actual work example as the means for demonstrating the family group manager's use of a variety of facilitation tools, techniques, and processes presented throughout this book.

➤ To highlight the power of secondary facilitation in action.

INTRODUCTION

The case you are about to read is the actual transcript of a meeting involving Al, the family group manager, and his seven direct reports. This particular meeting is a follow-up to one held the previous week in which the same group more or less decided to hold a team-building session for itself. The consequences of that nebulous decision will be felt in this meeting.

As you read this case, notice that Al demonstrates a process that allows him to function both in the role of primary facilitator and, when needed, in the role of active group participant.

At no time does Al abdicate the role prescribed by the formal organization—the role of manager of the group.

The case also shows facilitation as a shared responsibility. Thus, people other than Al demonstrate good facilitation skills as the group members share responsibility for successful facilitation. However, they are not perfect; mistakes will be made.

Finally, I have included my comments next to the group dialogue as a way to bridge back to key learning points from the previous chapters. My intent is to hit the highlights and to briefly note some of the more subtle interactions. You are urged to dig deeper and look for understanding and learning beyond my points. Have fun with this case. Pretend you are sitting in a corner watching this group operate. What do you see? What feedback would you give the group members regarding things they did well? In order to improve, what would you challenge them to do differently next time?

"To Team-Build or Not to Team-Build? That Is the Question"

Al: Okay. Well, I'm glad we were all able to get together today given our hectic travel schedules and workload. [While flipping back a blank page to reveal a pre-written flip chart page. Al points to the different items as he continues to speak.] The purpose of today's session is: To share and process information relative to holding an off-site team-building session for ourselves. The desired outcome is: Team-building go/no go consensus decision made. Regarding roles, I'll be the primary facilitator for this meeting; the rest of you, of course, have the role of secondary facilitators. Kathy,

A model beginning. The purpose, desired outcome, role assignments, and agenda all were pre-written, posted, and reviewed before any other business was transacted.

would you take the minutes and note all decisions plus any action items that arise? [She nods in agreement.] Also, Andrea, would you be the timekeeper? We would like to be finished in thirty minutes.

Andrea: Fine, no problem.

Al: Good, you'll see on the agenda that the first twenty minutes is allotted to examining the logistics and the pros and cons of holding a team-building session. The last ten minutes will be used to make our decision. Any issues with the purpose, desired outcome, roles, or agenda for this session?

Checking back with the group to make sure everyone is on-board and committed to the meeting's direction. Anyone with a differing perspective has an opportunity to speak up.

Everyone: Looks good, fine, let's go, etc.

Al: Okay, I think it's going to be easy to tie down the loose ends from the team-building discussion we had at last Monday's staff meeting. I think we're pretty well in agreement on most of the particulars. One new point to add is that Ike Delock, the vice president of human resources, has sort of invited himself to sit in on this, and I said okay.

Uh oh. This substantially changes the situation. Al has made an autocratic, unilateral decision on an issue that has ramifications for the whole group. This was not his decision to make alone. Al would have been better off telling Ike he first would have to run it by the family group members to see if they approved of having Ike at the team-building session. Well, it's too late now. Let's see how the group responds to Al's pronouncement.

Diane: Oh, good!

Supporting.

Tom: [With anger] You've got to be kidding me! I don't want Ike to be there.

Feelings, disagreement. How will this be handled?

Bob: Why not? What's the problem with him?

Good secondary facilitation. Direct question, seeking information, trying to understand.

Tom: [In a sharp tone of voice] Because he is not part of our group. He's an outsider.

Still in feelings. Notice at this point Al has not said anything. He has not gotten defensive or argumentative, even though he precipitated the discussion and was directly challenged by Tom.

Diane: Well, Tom, I might look at that a little differently. Maybe it's an opportunity to develop a little openness and trust vertically rather than just between ourselves.

Disagreeing. Opinion giving. Trying to counteract feelings with logic. Even though Diane might have a good point, this argument is not going to convince Tom to change his mind since he is in the "feelings" stage.

Andrea: I agree with Tom. This workshop could be important to us as a family group.

Supporting.

Tom: Thank you.

He shows appreciation for Andrea's support.

Andrea: Having an outsider there could completely destroy it.

Opinion giving.

Kathy: But Andrea and Tom, there are pluses and minuses to this. It could go either way. I think we should talk about it a little. Let's explore it. What do you think Jeanne?

Good secondary facilitation. Harmonizing by proposing that communications be kept open and that the group take a balanced view. Good use of a direct question to gate-open for Jeanne.

Jeanne: Well, do you know Ike?

Direct question. Seeking information.

Tom: [With exasperation] No, I don't know him.

Giving information.

Jeanne: Super person. Really, I think he might . . . He's got a lot of skills, and I think he just really wants to observe our process.

Jeanne is selling. She's trying to convince Tom that Ike is "a good guy." This is not doing what is needed most right now—to clarify and better understand what Tom feels and why.

Tom: [With a burst of anger] Fine. I don't have anything against the man personally, but I just don't want to have a corporate spy in our midst!

Strong feelings. The anger is backed by a highly negative label—"corporate spy."

Kathy: Spying! That's pretty heavy duty, Tom. I don't know if I'd really want to put it that way.

Opinion giving. Kathy is not helping the situation at this moment. She is evaluating Tom's feelings ("pretty heavy duty" and "I wouldn't put it that way"). Kathy has a right to her feelings. However, she needs to make it clear to Tom she understands what he feels, and why, before stating her contrary views.

This is a common problem when feelings arise. People jump in and basically tell the person "you shouldn't feel your way" (which is wrong) "you should feel my way" (which is right). Al or someone else must step in soon and do what needs to be done: Try understanding what Tom feels, and why, rather than evaluating his feelings.

Tom: [Heatedly, with emphasis on the word "I"] Well, I would put it that way. Who put you in charge of what I think?

Defensive. An attack on Kathy. The group is on the verge of destructive conflict.

Ron: Do you really feel like he is going to be spying or . . .

Excellent secondary facilitation. Ron does exactly what is needed at exactly the right time. He tests comprehension by trying to understand Tom's feelings. He gets gate closed before he can finish.

Tom: [In a much calmer voice] Well, spying . . . Maybe I'm saying more that he would just inhibit our freedom to speak up amongst ourselves.

Information giving, very useful insight to Tom's feelings. Ron's probe has helped settle him down.

Ron: Well I can certainly understand how Ike's presence could hinder our communications, but I'd like to follow up on Diane's point about the vertical slice . . .

Ron supports Tom and then shifts to harmonizing to look at Diane's side of the coin.

Some things to note: Al has not said anything. However, throughout this skirmish, his nonverbal cues indicated rapt attention to what was going on. He was fully in charge. He was mentally monitoring everything. Had Ron not clarified Tom's feelings when he did, Al would have had to intervene and do so. The point is, Al was waiting. He was staying out of the content and monitoring the process. Remember, just because you are the primary facilitator, doesn't mean you have to actively facilitate if you are getting good secondary facilitation. Al was receiving good facilitation support so he waited, he watched, he listened, he monitored.

Diane: Yes, and even take the word "spy." You can turn that over and look at the other side. He has an ear to the top. In watching our processes, he can relay back that we are doing pretty good. Also, he can see first hand what problems are caused by some of the mandates that come down from "on high." Why, you remember last year when they changed that hiring procedure? It took us six months to get things rolling again. Why, the first few days I had fifty phone calls . . .

Diane grabs the little opening provided by Ron by gate closing him to explain the merits of her position. However, notice that she begins to ramble and starts getting "revved up" on an unrelated tangent, the hiring procedure.

Al: Help me understand how that's going to help us move ahead with this issue.

Firm, but friendly confrontation. Al steps in to gate close Diane's unproductive rambling.

Diane: Well, if Ike had been there, perhaps some action could have been taken in six weeks, not six months. I see that as a positive aspect of his presence.

Diane stops rambling and crisply explains her position.

Ron: So you think Ike should be at the workshop? [Diane nods in agreement.] Tom?

Direct question, testing comprehension, gate opening for Tom.

Tom: [In a conciliatory tone] I don't think that if we are going to try to pull together as a team we need any outsiders looking at our team process at this stage of the game. While I appreciate Diane's position, I can't agree that this should be a vertical workshop. I don't see it that way.

Tom now states the issue in situational rather than behavioral terms. **He is starting the transition from feelings to facts.**

Ron: Would you participate in the workshop or . . .

Seeking information, still trying to fully understand Tom's perspective.

Tom: [Forcefully, but without anger] I guess, answering the question: If Ike's going to be there, I don't think that I would show up.

Giving information. Strong message indicating how deeply Tom feels about this being only a family group team building with no outsiders.

Bob: [Irritated] Wait a minute. Wait a minute. At our last staff meeting we had decided exactly what we were going to do. We knew we were going to do this thing. We had reached consensus. Everybody agreed. And here we are rehashing the same thing over again. We simply won't take "yes" for an answer. Diane, you were given the action item for pulling this thing off. What is it that we decided?

Mini feelings. Giving information, summarizing points from previous staff meeting. Direct question to gate open for Diane. Actually a good piece of secondary facilitation.

Even though there are divergent views, the group is now working at processing information. Communications are open; there are no personal attacks, there is no destructive conflict at this time. The group is starting to problem-solve. **It has moved into the "facts" phase.**

Diane: Well, if we're getting back to asking the question of what were our goals, maybe we weren't exactly clear enough about that. I think maybe we all assumed that we knew what was our top priority, or what the possibilities were, and maybe we didn't take that far enough.

Opinion giving. But more importantly, Diane has uncovered the root of the conflict: lack of good clarity about the intent of the team-building workshop at the close of the previous meeting. A major breakthrough.

Andrea: As timekeeper I'd like to interject a quick performance check and remind everyone that we are half-way through our session and there are fifteen more minutes to go.

Performance checking, giving information to assist the group process.

Ron: Thanks, Andrea, that Rolex keeps good time.

Andrea: At $29.95 it had better. [The group laughs.]

A tension-relieving exchange. Nothing boisterous, well-timed, a brief interlude to inject a bit of levity.

Ron: Getting back to our team-building issue, I think both Tom and Diane raise good points. I also think Bob's got a good point on the process itself that we used last week. Al, you've been silent on this one so far. You've talked to Ike personally about coming down. What's your position on having him participate?

Encouraging. Another piece of good secondary facilitation by Ron. He also uses a direct question to gate open and draw Al into the content side of the discussion. It's perfectly proper for a subordinate to draw the manager into the discussion, if there is a felt need to do so.

Al: Well, first let me take off my facilitator's hat and look at it from the role of a family group manager. I . . . obviously, he [Ike] pointed out to me that he would like to invite himself and I said "Sure, come on in." I was pretty comfortable with it. I don't feel threatened by it. I may be the farthest in the spectrum away from Tom's position in terms of comfort in seeing him join us. I don't have any issue with that. On the other hand, when I put my facilitator's hat back on, and I listen to the issue from Tom's perspective, I hear the "other voices." It may be that where we really got off was that when we were discussing this and planning it, we weren't very

Now we'll see the substantial benefits of a manager who stayed out of the content but was totally tuned in to the group process through listening and mentally monitoring the dynamics.

Al does a nice job of signifying his shift in roles by "hat switching." He does a superb job of summarizing the main issues and clarifying his personal position. Notice, that everything Al says is stated in situational, not behavioral terms. He defines Ike's role under two different goal conditions. Al gets to the heart of the problem and clarifies its essence: by first determining the goal of the team-building session, clear about our goals. We said "I've got a great idea. Let's have a family group meeting, a team-building session." But we may not have identified what it was that we wanted to accomplish with that. I think that, on the one hand, if it's to improve our facilitation skills as a team then Ike's an outsider and an interloper, and he probably isn't a contributor. He's certainly not a key person. On the other hand, if the purpose of the team-building session is to improve our relationship with corporate human resources, then Ike becomes a key player. And so we've got a lack of clarity in our goals, or, at least, we haven't set them in place. Maybe we ought to test and see what kind of consensus we've got on the goal of team-building. Maybe that's where we ought to begin. Let's test the alternative that this should be a family group team-building session. Kathy, how do you feel about this?

Kathy: I would agree that it should be a family group team-building session.

Al: Okay, Bob?

Bob: I agree. Family group only.

Tom: Family group.

Andrea: Family group.

the staff then will have defined Ike's role of either being involved and not involved.

Addressing the goal issue, Al now performs the consensus-testing activity by asking each person, in turn, if he or she can support the goal of the team-building as being a family group session. **Al has moved the team into the "solutions" phase.**

229

Ron: I think family group. I think it's important that we do ourselves first before we start bringing in other people. I think Tom's got a good point.

Jeanne: That's our goal. I agree.

Al: Okay. Diane?

Diane: Well, I still think that optimally we could get both out of the same session. But if what you're saying to me, Tom, is that you don't think that we could, and you're forcing me into a choice, well, the choice is an easy choice because I would much rather have your input into our team-building session than Ike's.

Opinion giving. Diane reiterates her original position and then supports the consensus of the group. The word "forcing" does leave some doubt that she truly is committed to a family group session.

Jeanne: Diane, you said Tom was forcing you into your choice. So you feel pressured?

Summarizing followed by an excellent example of testing comprehension. Jeanne picked up on the word "forcing" and checked to see if that is what Diane really meant. A critical piece of secondary facilitation.

Diane: Oh, no, no, that's not what I meant. It was a poor choice of words. I fully support having this be a family group session. My arm's not being twisted.

Information giving to clarify her position. We know now that Diane really is behind the family group team-building idea.

Al: Okay, I also agree that we make this a family group session. So what we're really saying, then, is that we've got a two-step plan. Our goal first of all is to improve our own family group facilitation skills. And if that's our goal, that makes Ike an outsider, and we probably ought to note that this is where we are headed, and we probably ought to uninvite Ike. And then we have a secondary issue, which is that at some point we want to address the goal of upward facilitation and interface with human resources. And if that's the case, then Ike moves from being a peripheral player to being a key person. We will want to address that down the road.

Al gives his consent last. He waited so as not to unduly influence the group.
Al summarizes what was agreed to and also takes steps to make this a win/win outcome by offering the option of holding a team-building session with Ike after this one. Diane can still meet her original goal with Al's proposal. This will cement her commitment even more. The group has reached a true consensus. Everyone has verbally acknowledged that they either "agree with" or "agree to support" the idea of a family group session as their first team-building activity.

Tom: Good.

Diane: Let's do it.

Ron: Fine, that leaves just one last thing regarding the action item that Kathy is putting in the minutes. Who is going to call Ike?

General address question. Nice piece of secondary facilitation to make sure all action items are "buttoned up."

Al: Tom, do you want to do it? Do you want me to do it?

Direct question. A curious statement. Why would Al ask Tom if he wanted to call Ike? Tom wasn't the one who invited Ike.

Tom: I think you can do that.

What would you expect him to say?

Al: No problem. I think that's fine. Well, that's an interesting one. Somewhere along the line last week we made a classic assumption in terms of what the goal was and slid right by it. I think we all learned something by that. Bob, as a first step in planning for our team-building session, would you check out the prices for room rentals and food at several local hotels and report back with options at our next staff meeting on the 22nd?

Solid wrap-up and close.

Bob: Will do.

Al: Finally, here is a copy of the "Group Session Effectiveness Evaluation" that we have been using to critique our meetings. Please fill it out and give it to Kathy so she can put the results in our minutes. We'll discuss any issues on the 22nd.

The road to managing conflict and strong feelings is rarely smooth or straight. As this case illustrates, it requires a team effort to work through diversity. Al, acting as primary facilitator, in combination with other group members performing as secondary facilitators, practiced a number of tools, techniques, and processes for "mining group gold." Doing so enabled them to turn a potentially explosive situation into one that reached a productive conclusion. The team was able to discover that the true source of conflict and feelings was its collective failure to define the team-building goals at the end of the previous week's staff meeting. Once the real conflict was identified, the group took action to resolve it. In doing so, the team proceeded along the "feelings, facts, solutions" sequence to group productivity.

A CONCLUDING THOUGHT

Will Rogers once said of Congress: "When all is said and done, a lot more is said than done." Often that is the case with planning and facilitating group sessions—people say a lot about what needs to be done, but they do little in the way of changing and improving. I hope this book will give you the confidence and ability to become a true "miner of group gold" so that "When all is said and done, a lot less will be said and a lot more collaboration will be done."

As I wrote in the preface, "Without your desire to use them, the ideas presented here are useless. You are completely in charge of what these ideas will ultimately mean to you and your organization."

Notes Worksheet: DEVELOP WRITTEN RESPONSES TO THE TWO ITEMS LISTED BELOW

What do you feel are the main learning points from Chapter 10?	Elaborate on why you feel these points are key.

REFERENCES ON GROUP SESSION FACILITATION, TEAMWORK, AND COLLABORATION

VIDEO

Mining Group Gold: The Quality Approach to Group Interaction. Carlsbad, CA: CRM Films, 1992, 1-800-421-0833.

BOOKS

Albrecht, K., and S. Albrecht. *Added Value Negotiating: The Breakthrough Method for Building Balanced Deals.* Burr Ridge, IL: Irwin Professional Publishing, 1993.

Auvine, B., B. Densmore, M. Extrom, S. Poole, and M. Shanklin. *A Manual for Group Facilitators.* Madison, WI: The Center for Conflict Resolution, 1978.

Avery, M., B. Auvine, B. Streibel, and L. Weiss. *Building United Judgment: A Handbook for Consensus Decision Making.* Madison, WI: The Center for Conflict Resolution, 1981.

Bell, A. H. *Mastering the Meeting Maze.* Reading, MA: Addison-Wesley, 1990.

Bradford, L. P., ed. *Group Development*, 2d ed. San Diego, CA: Pfeiffer & Company, 1978.

Bradford, L. P. *Making Meetings Work.* La Jolla, CA: University Associates, 1976.

Butman, J. *Flying Fox: A Business Adventure in Teams and Teamwork.* New York: AMACOM, 1993.

Daniels, W. R. *Group Power I: A Manager's Guide to Using Task Force Meetings.* San Diego, CA: Pfeiffer & Company, 1986.

Daniels, W. R. *Group Power II: A Manager's Guide to Conducting Regular Meetings*. San Diego, CA: Pfeiffer & Company, 1990.

Dimock, H. G. *Groups: Leadership and Group Development*. San Diego, CA: Pfeiffer & Company, 1987.

Dimock, H. G. *Intervention and Collaboration: Helping Organizations to Change*. San Diego, CA: Pfeiffer & Company, 1993.

Doyle, M., and D. Straus. *How to Make Meetings Work: The New Interaction Method*. New York: Berkley Publishing Group, 1976.

Frank, M. O. *How to Run a Meeting in Half the Time*. New York: Simon and Schuster, 1989.

Grove, A. S. "Meetings—The Medium of Managerial Work," in *High Output Management*. New York: Vintage Books, 1985.

Haynes, M. E. *Effective Meeting Skills: A Practical Guide for More Productive Meetings*. Menlo Park, CA: Crisp Publications, 1988.

Hirschhorn, L. *Managing in the New Team Environment*. Reading, MA: Addison-Wesley, 1991.

Katzenbach, J. R., and D. K. Smith. *The Wisdom of Teams: Creating the High Performance Organization*. Boston: Harvard Business School Press, 1993.

Kayser, T. A. *Building Team Power: How to Unleash the Collaborative Genius of Work Teams*. Burr Ridge, IL: Irwin Professional Publishing, 1994.

Kieffer, G. D. *The Strategy of Meetings*. New York: Simon and Schuster, 1988.

Kindler, H. S. *Managing Disagreement Constructively*. Menlo Park, CA: Crisp Publications, 1988.

Kinlaw, D. C. *Team Managed Facilitation*. San Diego, CA: Pfeiffer & Company, 1993.

Lipnack, J., and J. Stamps. *The TeamNet Factor: Bringing the Power of Boundary Crossing into the Heart of Your Business*. Essex Junction, VT: Oliver Wright Publications, 1993.

Maier, N. R. F. *Problem-Solving Discussions and Conferences*. New York: McGraw-Hill, 1963.

Martin, C. L., and D. Hackett. *Facilitation Skills for Team Leaders*. Menlo Park, CA: Crisp Publications, 1992.

Mosvick, R. K., and R. B. Nelson. *We've Got to Start Meeting Like This!* Glenview, IL: Scott, Foresman, 1987.

Parker, G. M. *Cross-Functional Teams: Working with Allies, Enemies, and Other Strangers*. San Francisco: Jossey-Bass, 1994.

Sayles, L., and G. Strauss. "Conference Leadership," in *Human Behavior in Organizations.* Englewood Cliffs, NJ: Prentice-Hall, 1966.

Schein, E. H. *Process Consultation: Its Role in Organizational Development,* vol. 1, 2d ed. Reading, MA: Addison-Wesley, 1988.

Schein, E. H. *Process Consultation: Lessons for Managers and Consultants,* vol. 2. Reading, MA: Addison-Wesley, 1987.

Schlinder-Rainman, E., and R. Lippit. *Taking Your Meetings Out of the Doldrums.* San Diego, CA: Pfeiffer & Company, 1977.

Schmidt, W. H., and J. P. Finnigan. *TQM Manager: A Practical Guide for Managing in a Total Quality Organization.* San Francisco: Jossey-Bass, 1993.

Shonk, J. H. *Team-Based Organizations: Developing a Successful Team Environment.* Burr Ridge, IL: Irwin Professional Publishing, 1992.

Tagliere, D. A. *How to Meet, Think, and Work to Consensus.* San Diego, CA: Pfeiffer & Company, 1992.

The 3M Meeting Management Team. *How to Run Better Business Meetings: A Reference Guide for Managers.* New York: McGraw-Hill, 1987.

Thomsett, M. C. *The Little Black Book of Business Meetings.* New York: AMACOM, 1989.

Tjosvold, D. *Teamwork for Customers: Building Organizations that Take Pride in Serving.* San Francisco: Jossey-Bass, 1993.

Walton, R. E. *Managing Conflict: Interpersonal Dialogue and Third Party Roles,* 2d ed. Reading, MA: Addison-Wesley, 1987.

Wood, J. T., G. M. Phillips, and D. J. Pederson. *Group Discussion: A Practical Guide to Participation and Leadership.* 2d ed. New York: Harper and Row, 1986.

Zander, A. *Making Groups Effective.* San Francisco, CA: Jossey-Bass, 1983.

Zenger, J. H., E. Musselwhite, K. Hurson, C. Perrin. *Leading Teams: Mastering the New Role.* Burr Ridge, IL: Irwin Professional Publishing, 1994.

RESEARCH REPORTS

Cohen, S. G. *Teams and Teamwork: Future Directions,* Center for Effective Organizations, University of Southern California, G91-9 (194), 1991.

Mohrman, Jr., A. M., S. A. Mohrman, E. E. Lawler, III. *The Performance Management of Teams,* Center for Effective Organizations, University of Southern California, G91-2 (187), 1991.

Monge, P. R., C. McSween, J. Wyer. *A Profile of Meetings in Corporate America: Results of the 3M Effectiveness Study,* Annenberg School of Communications, University of Southern California, November 1989.

Oppenheim, L. *Making Meetings Matter: A Report to the 3M Corporation,* Wharton Center for Applied Research, 1987.

Rudzinski, J. E. *The Intelligent Company: Corporate Change through Collective Meaning,* SRI International, Report No. 831, Fall 1994.

ARTICLES

Anfuso, D. "Xerox Partners with the Union to Regain Market Share," *Personnel Journal,* August 1994.

Barkan, P. "Strategic and Tactical Benefits of Simultaneous Engineering," *Design Management Journal,* Spring 1991, pp. 39–42.

Byrne, J. A. "The Horizontal Corporation," *Business Week,* December 20, 1993, pp. 76–81.

Deutschman, A. "The Managing Wisdom of High-Tech Superstars," *Fortune,* October 17, 1994, pp. 197–206.

Dumaine, B. "The Bureaucracy Busters," *Fortune,* June 17, 1991, pp. 36–50.

English, G. "How about a Good Word for Meetings," *Management Review,* June 1990, pp. 58–60.

Green, W. A., and H. Lazarus. "Are Today's Executives Meeting with Success," *Journal of Management Development,* Vol. 10, No. 1, 1991, pp. 14–25.

Huey, J. "The New Post-Heroic Leadership," *Fortune,* February 21, 1994, pp. 42–50.

Johnson, V. "Emotional Rescue: What to Do When Bad Feelings Happen in Good Groups," *Successful Meetings,* January 1992, pp. 142–144.

Kanter, R. M. "The Collaborative Advantage: The Art of Alliances," *Harvard Business Review,* July–August 1994, pp. 96–108.

Lorenz, R. A. "Team-Based Engineering at Deere," *The McKinsey Quarterly,* Number 4, 1991, pp. 81–93.

Lutz, R. A. "Implementing Technological Change with Cross-Functional Teams," *Research Technology Management*, March–April 1994, pp. 14–18.

Montebello, A. R., V. R. Buzzotta. "Work Teams that Work," *Training and Development Journal*, March 1993, pp. 59–64.

Orlin, J. M. "Selling in Teams," *Training and Development Journal*, December 1993, pp. 26–32.

Parker, G. M. "Cross Functional Collaboration," *Training and Development Journal*, October 1994, pp. 49–53.

Rapaport, R. "To Build a Winning Team: An Interview with Head Coach Bill Walsh," *Harvard Business Review*, January–February 1993, pp. 111–120.

Ray, G. R., J. Hines, and D. Wilcox. "Training Internal Facilitators," *Training and Development Journal*, November 1994, pp. 45–48.

The 3M Meeting Management Institute. "Facilitation: Meeting Leadership Style for the '90s," *Meeting Management News*, Vol. 3, No. 3, December 1991, pp. 2–4.

Tobia, P. M., and M. C. Becker. "Making the Most of Meeting Time," *Training and Development Journal*, August 1990, pp. 34–38.

INTERESTED IN A

MINING GROUP GOLD® *WORKSHOP*

FOR YOUR ORGANIZATION?

For more information on a *sixteen hour*, highly interactive, skill building workshop linked directly to the material presented in Tom Kayser's best selling book, please call:

Carol Kayser, President

Kayser Associates

62 Deer Creek Rd.

Pittsford, NY 14534

(716) 586 - 2327

All of the workshop's simulations and structured experiences are designed to insure that learning application takes place within a supportive environment. Every module provides time to directly interact with Carol Kayser, your workshop facilitator, to review, question, and absorb the techniques and processes presented in *Mining Group Gold.* The single goal is to help you and your team members become confident "miners of group gold." Workshops are delivered at a site of your choosing; and, based on your needs, can be formatted to be longer or shorter than the standard sixteen hour workshop.

INDEX

Other Books of interest to you . . .

BUILDING TEAM POWER
How to Unleash the Collaborative Genius of Work Teams
Thomas A. Kayser

Building Team Power offers easy-to-implement ideas, tools, and techniques for increasing team productivity in an environment, whether public or private sector, profit or nonprofit, or service- or manufacturing-based.
ISBN: 0-7863-0302-6

DIVERSE TEAMS AT WORK
Capitalizing on the Power of Diversity
Lee Gardenswartz and Anita Rowe

Diverse Teams at Work shows how to manage the many differences inherent to today's teams, and provides an analysis of the primary dimensions of diversity and how they shape expectations and team behavior.
ISBN: 0-7863-0425-1

WHY TEAMS CAN FAIL AND WHAT TO DO ABOUT IT
Essential Tools for Anyone Implementing Self-Directed Work Teams
Darcy Hitchcock and Marsha Willard

Why Teams Can Fail identifies the most common problems faced by teams, offering specific suggestions for spotting and solving the problems and creating teams that really work.
ISBN: 0-7863-0423-5

Also available in fine bookstores and libraries everywhere.